# The Police–Mental Health Partnership

STEVEN MARANS

in collaboration with

JEAN ADNOPOZ

MIRIAM BERKMAN

DEAN ESSERMAN

DOUGLAS MACDONALD

STEVEN NAGLER

RICHARD RANDALL

MARK SCHAEFER

MELVIN WEARING

Yale University Press  New Haven and London

# The
# Police-Mental Health
# Partnership A Community-Based
Response to Urban Violence

This manual was prepared with support from the United States Department of Justice, Office of Juvenile Justice and Delinquency Prevention (OJJDP).

This document was produced under grant no. 93–JN–CX–0004 from the United States Department of Justice, Office of Juvenile Justice and Delinquency Prevention. Points of view or opinions expressed in this document are those of the authors and do not necessarily represent the official positions or policies of the OJJDP.

Designed by Nancy Ovedovitz. Set in Galliard type by Keystone Typesetting, Inc. Printed in the United States of America by BookCrafters, Inc., Chelsea, Michigan.

Library of Congress Cataloging-in-Publication Data

Marans, Steven.
The police mental health partnership : a community-based response to urban violence / Steven Marans in collaboration with Jean Adnopoz . . . (el al.].
  p.  cm.
  Includes bibliographical references (p.   ) and index.
  ISBN 0–300–06420–9 (alk. paper)
  1. Community policing — Connecticut — New Haven.   2. Problem families — Connecticut — New Haven.   3. Mental health personnel — Training of — Connecticut — New Haven.   4. Police — Training of — Connecticut — New Haven.   I. Adnopoz, Jean. II. Title.
HV7936.C83M27   1995
363.2'3'097468 — dc20                       95–18519
                                                            CIP

A catalogue record for this book is available from the British Library.

The paper in this book meets the guidelines for permanence and durability of the Committee on Production Guidelines for Book Longevity of the Council on Library Resources.

10      9      8      7      6      5      4      3      2      1

# Contents

**Foreword** vii

**The Authors** xi

**Acknowledgments** xiii

1 **Introduction** 1
Exposure to Community Violence, 2    Community
Policing, 5    Community Mental Health, 8
A Collaborative Response to Urban Violence, 10
Program Components, 11    The Experience of
Collaboration, 16

2  **Child Development Fellowships  19**
Selection of Participants, 24    Fellowship Training, 27
Issues Raised by the Fellowship Collaboration, 33

3  **Training Seminars  40**
Seminar Outline, 42    1. Introduction, 2. Infancy,
3. Separation and Trauma, 4. Young Children, 5. School-Age
Children, 6. Puberty and Early Adolescence, 7. Issues of
Race and Socioeconomic Status, 8. Adolescence,
9. Conclusion

4  **Consultation Service  62**
Basic Elements of the Consultation Service, 63
Guidelines for Operating a Consultation Service, 71

5  **Program Conference  84**
Case Review, 86    Integration and Application, 93
Systemic and Institutional Issues, 94
Administration, 95

6  **Program Development  96**
Phase 1: Institutional Investment, 97    Phase 2: Initial
Program Development, 97    Phase 3: Implementation, 99
Data and Records, 99    Budgetary Considerations, 100

7  **Results of the New Haven Program  104**
Changes in Police Practice, 105    Changes in Clinical
Practice, 109    Clinical Findings, 111    Case Illustrations, 113
Discussion, 122

**Appendix  125**
Yale Child Study Center Post-Traumatic Stress Questionnaire
Parent Form, 125    Child Development–Community Policing
Program Introductory Report, 130    Child Development–
Community Policing Program Monthly Case Service Log, 138

**References  139**

**Index  143**

# Foreword

Several years ago, a group of faculty in the Yale Child Study Center became more immersed in thinking about the pathways into violence and the large number of children in clinical services whose lives were burdened by aggression. At the same time, police in New Haven embarked on a new, community-based approach that relied on the development of relationships between officers and the neighborhood residents for whom they work. In both fields, it became clear that we had to find other approaches to being useful, to augment traditional policing and clinical responses with more sustained and systemic interventions in the lives of children and families at risk. At this time, we met with each other and recognized our shared concern about the same groups of children and families — children who presented themselves to the police because their families or they were involved with violence and who came to the attention of clinicians as traumatized, anxious, and angry youngsters who defied attempts at treatment. These were the children, most often children of color, on our street corners, in the mall, suspended or truant from school, and the tougher and more beaten-down youth whose future entry into jobs and careers was threatened by poor skills or by the scars of drugs and gang warfare. We saw these children from different perspectives; yet, remarkably, we were completely synchronized in our understanding of their development and their needs. Discussions among us and our colleagues led to the Child Development–Community Policing Program.

Discussions between police and psychiatrists and psychologists are not an academic luxury. Today, mental health professionals must become familiar with the goals, procedures, and philosophy of police departments because law enforcement officers are so involved with their child patients. In addition, clinicians will learn about the important role that police play in stabilizing communities and how individual officers may serve not only as the authoritative voice of the larger society providing structure but also as the thoughtful, compassionate professional available to children involved in trauma.

On the other side, police officers need to be prepared for the new responsibilities of community-based policing. The early detection of children on their way to trouble, of children who have experienced traumatic situations, of recurrent problems in families, of the absence of preventative health care, places burdens on police officers. The new officer has a preventive role and an early intervention responsibility; the officer does not consider himself or

herself successful through making more arrests but through helping to reduce crime, diverting children from adverse outcomes,
and helping the victims, and not simply capturing the villains.
Where will police officers learn about children and families and
acquire a kind of "clinical" understanding to carry out the expanded, neighborhood-based responsibilities more effectively?

The New Haven model is a bridge of collaboration. Through
the program, mental health professionals learn from police officers
about the broad social context, the nature of the communities and
families, the texture of children's lives, and the immediate circumstances that are traumatic and the stimulus for their involvement.
They also learn about the steps leading to violence and the aftermath. In turn, police learn from mental health professionals about
the preconditions for healthy development, the impact of trauma
and stress, the process of recovery, and the emergence of patholog-
ical patterns of adaptation. Together, police and mental health professionals can learn how to mobilize treatment services more
quickly and effectively and how to assure that treatment plans are
carried out.

Child mental health workers cannot afford to ignore the powerful role of police for many patients and groups of patients, nor can
police officers simply go on their own in intervening in these most
complicated situations. Dr. Marans and his colleagues bring community-based policing and their model of collaboration to life. The
program already has had a national impact on services and plans,
and this volume will help bring the work and the details of how it
can be implemented to many other communities and to other professionals who are deeply concerned about children and families.

DONALD J. COHEN, M.D.,                        NICHOLAS PASTORE,
*Director and Irving B. Harris Professor of Child Psychiatry,*   *Chief, New Haven*
*Psychology, and Pediatrics, Child Study Center,*    *Department of Police Service*
*Yale University School of Medicine*

# The Authors

JEAN ADNOPOZ, M.P.H., associate clinical professor and coordinator of community child development and child welfare programs, Child Study Center, Yale University School of Medicine
MIRIAM BERKMAN, J.D., M.S.W., assistant clinical professor in social work, Child Study Center, Yale University School of Medicine
DEAN ESSERMAN, J.D., Chief, Metropolitan Transit Authority, Metro-North Police, formerly assistant chief, New Haven Department of Police Service
LIEUTENANT DOUGLAS MACDONALD, New Haven Department of Police Service

STEVEN MARANS, M.S.W., Ph.D., coordinator, Child Development–Community Policing Program, and Harris Assistant Professor of Child Psychoanalysis, Child Study Center, Yale University School of Medicine

STEVEN NAGLER, M.S.W., assistant clinical professor in social work, Child Study Center, Yale University School of Medicine

SERGEANT RICHARD RANDALL, New Haven Department of Police Service

MARK SCHAEFER, Ph.D., associate research scientist, Child Study Center, Yale University School of Medicine

MELVIN WEARING, Assistant Chief, New Haven Department of Police Service

# Acknowledgments

The Child Development–Community Policing Program was generated by the vision and leadership of Nicholas Pastore, Chief of the New Haven Department of Police Service, and Donald J. Cohen, Director of the Child Study Center, Yale University School of Medicine. Their shared concerns about the children and families exposed to community violence have paved the way to new partnerships and new solutions. We are grateful to the Rockefeller Foundation, the Smart Family Foundation, the B'nai B'rith Women, and an anonymous donor for their support and to the U.S. Department of Justice Office of Juvenile Justice and Delinquency Prevention for funding the preparation of this manual. We are indebted to Sergeant Vaughn Maher (retired) and Sergeant Marshall Gambrell for their leadership and contribution to the development of the program and to our close colleagues, Steven Berkowitz, M.D., James Canning, M.S.W., Robert King, M.D., Sergeant Herman Badger, Sergeant Donald Celmer, and Sergeant Anthony Griego, as well as to the many police officers and clinicians who have responded to the children and families in need and have been our teachers. We are especially grateful to our esteemed colleague and teacher, Alice Colonna, a senior child analyst at the Child Study Center. In addition, we are grateful for the invaluable assistance of Pat Santoro, Colleen Vadala, Margrethe Cone, and Mary Jane Chicoski in completing this work.

The Police-Mental Health Partnership

STEVEN MARANS

MIRIAM BERKMAN

DEAN ESSERMAN

# 1   Introduction

Today, when the threat and reality of violence overwhelm whole communities and undermine the sense of safety that is crucial to the optimal development and realization of the potential of our children, it is time to rethink the ways in which we intervene on their behalf. The Child Development–Community Policing (CD-CP) Program outlined in this manual aims to capitalize on the interests of two groups of professionals who have long been concerned about children caught in the cross fire of community violence but who, until recently, have worked in isolation. The collaboration between mental health and police professionals described in this manual was born out of a commonsense recognition that, when properly equipped, police officers are in a unique position to affect the lives of children and families who are at greatest risk of becoming the psychological casualties of violence. Similarly, when mental health professionals venture beyond the consulting room, they are in a much stronger position to intervene before exposure to violence leads to the perpetration of violence.

The Child Development–Community Policing Program capitalizes on the fact that police make house calls twenty-four hours a day. Joining forces not only reintroduces this approach to mental health professionals but also is consistent with their recognition that proactive response to emotional trauma in the wake of community violence both broadens traditional clinical services and diminishes the severity of long-term effects of exposure to violence on children and families. When officers are properly trained and supported, their roles in the lives of children and families are similarly expanded. When officers recognize the emotional needs of children and have a clearer understanding of principles of human functioning, their sense of effectiveness is enhanced and their range of strategies for intervention is increased. When backup includes the ability to deliver psychological services to children and families and consultation about complex and at times dangerous behavior, officers' stature in the community climbs as figures of benign authority and as models for identification.

### EXPOSURE TO COMMUNITY VIOLENCE

The daily headlines in local newspapers and the grim reports on nightly news programs bring the drama and explosive nature of urban violence into the homes of all Americans. Many families who live in inner cities, however, do not need to turn on their television sets to experience the threat of violence. They hear the sound of gunfire nightly or witness shootings, stabbings, and fist-fights in their homes and streets; both the assailants and the victims are their relatives and neighbors.

Communal violence in the United States did not originate during the late twentieth century. However, today gangs fight not with fists, knives, and chains but with semiautomatic and automatic weapons. And the stakes are no longer determined by neighborhood pride, turf, and ethnic issues alone, but are driven by competitive market forces of a lucrative drug trade. Gone are the days of zip guns and Saturday night specials, replaced now by high-tech 14-shot handguns that can be rented by the hour. Unemployment, multigenerational poverty, and family dissolution contribute to a sense of helplessness and rage that — for many urban youth — can find a measure of relief in the power of fast money and the violent resolution of disputes. The combatants are not the only victims of violence. Whole communities, turned into captive observers, experience violence secondhand and worry about who will be the next intended or unintended casualty. The specter of violence, both real and threatened, can make overwhelming their feelings of impotence in the face of substandard housing, inadequate education, and the absence of jobs.

For children, the experience of acute, isolated episodes of violence often is superimposed on chronic exposure to violence. Specific incidents may lead to a range of emotional reactions, including symptoms of post-traumatic stress disorder — disrupted patterns of eating, sleeping, and paying attention and relating, as well as fearfulness, flashbacks, and the like (DSM-IV). Repeated exposure to violence may also lead to persistent patterns of psychological maladaptation. Children so exposed may withdraw, turn inward, and appear depressed; they may have difficulties with attention, school performance, and social engagement; they may instead become the aggressive perpetrator. By engaging in delinquent and violent activities, children who had been victims of community violence may now organize their sense of self around involvement in the type of experience that initially was so threatening. When a child is exposed to violence on a regular basis, identifying with the power and excitement of delinquent and violent role models may become a chronic hedge against feeling helpless and afraid. When the most powerful models in the home and neighborhood exercise their potency with a fist or a gun, the lure of violent and criminal activity may overcome the power and rewards in productive participation in the life of the community (Marans and Cohen, 1993).

The statistics regarding the incidence of assaultive violence are disturbing in and of themselves. From 1984 to 1993 there was a 51 percent increase in violent crimes (defined by Uniform Crime Reports as murder, forcible rape, robbery, and aggravated assault). In 1993 there were

- 24,526 murders
- 104,806 rapes
- 659,757 robberies
- 1,135,099 aggravated assaults.

Between 1984 and 1993 there was a 46.1 percent increase in arrests for possession of weapons (U.S. Department of Justice, 1994).

The potential number of children as psychological victims may far outnumber the medical casualties that reach our emergency rooms or the headlines of our newspapers. In New Haven, it is estimated that more than one-third of the children seen in the Child Study Center outpatient clinic have been exposed to aggression or involved in its consequences (P. Armbruster, personal communication). The number of children who actually receive psychological care, however, represents only a fraction of the most vulnerable in the population who are exposed to violence. For example, in a study conducted at Boston City Hospital, it was reported that one of every ten children seen in the primary care clinic had witnessed a shooting or stabbing before the age of six — half in the home, half on the streets. The average age of the children was 2.7 years (Taylor et al., in press). In a survey of fifth- and sixth-grade students in Washington, D.C., 31 percent reported having witnessed a shooting, 17 percent had witnessed a stabbing, 9 percent had witnessed a murder, and 23 percent had seen a dead body (Richters and Martinez, 1993). Children's greater exposure to violence was associated with increased self reports of depression and anxiety (Martinez and Richters, 1993). Similarly, in a study conducted in New Haven schools of sixth-, eighth-, and tenth-graders, 40 percent reported having witnessed at least one violent crime in the past year (New Haven Public Schools, 1992). By their teenage years, only a small minority of inner-city children have not been directly exposed to violence — at home, on the street, or in school. The majority report being afraid almost everywhere outside their homes, and many are fearful at home, as well.

### COMMUNITY POLICING

Criminal justice scholars and police observers have taken note of the transformation going on in policing throughout our nation's cities. George L. Kelling (1988a) has called it the "quiet revolution in American policing." The changes taking place are profound, and their effects will continue to be felt in the years ahead.

During the 1980s, the police began to ask some fundamental questions about the way they were doing business. The delivery of police service in urban areas had become high-speed, high-tech, anonymous, and tough. The neighborhood beat cop had long been replaced by the more efficient, more streamlined, professional law-enforcement officer. This new breed of police officer left the street corner to work in a patrol car with a partner, plugged into a central dispatch center by a sophisticated communications system. Requests for police service came to be viewed as an unending demand that needed to be handled quickly and efficiently, so that patrol units were not "out of service" too long handling any one incident, unavailable for random preventive patrol and for the next call in the queue. Yet this approach did not seem to be working. Every attempt by the police to staunch the demand for their services seemed to fail, and each year brought ever greater demand and records of ever greater police activity. Something had to change. To many people's surprise, what changed was police attitudes.

What the police discovered was that, in an effort to gain efficiency in responding to the growing demand on their services, they had, in fact, diminished whatever connections they had to the neighborhoods and communities they were sworn to serve and protect. Reliance on anonymity and rapid response had further decreased officers' ability to prevent or deter crime and to intervene early on, before developing problems took hold. As Lee Brown, Secretary of Drug Policy and former chief of police in New York City, Atlanta, and Houston, observed, "The police were not part of the community" but rather had grown "apart from it" (Brown, 1990).

In the context of this critique which developed in the 1980s, police began to rethink their fundamental relationship to the communities they served and to recognize the value of closer personal connections between police and neighborhood residents. They gradually embraced the concept — once found all too threatening — of working with communities in a new partnership to identify problems, potential hazards, and fears and work together toward solutions. The police moved back into the neighborhoods, bringing back beat cops and community substations. In turn, they enhanced community councils and citizen-police management teams, beat maintenance, and collaborative strategies; these problem-solving approaches supplemented traditional strategies such as police sweeps, tactical planning teams, and SWAT operations. Individual police officers returned to patrolling street corners, housing projects, and neighborhoods. Officers were allowed — and encouraged — to become part of the communities they were serving, to trust and become trusted, and to work with the citizens on their beats to improve the quality of life in the neighborhood (Goldstein, 1990; Kelling, 1988b).

The police also began to rethink the unending demand for police services, most frequently represented by citizen telephone calls to 911, not as discrete, independent incidents or service calls but rather as multiple symptoms representing more deeply rooted problems (Sparrow, Kennedy, and Moore, 1990; Eck and Spelman, 1987). The police began to discuss strategies focused on problem solving rather than incident response. Officers began to voice an interest in working on solutions, not just repeatedly reacting to symptoms (Geller, 1991; Goldstein, 1990).

In this community-based, collaborative setting, a new role and job description for police officers began to emerge. An emphasis on prevention, deterrence, and early intervention evolved naturally. Community organizing, networking, and social service referrals became necessary day-to-day skills for community police officers. Communities recognized that enforcing the law and apprehending offenders were only a part of what they wanted from officers and only part of what officers actually did (Goldstein, 1977).

The police are the major representatives of societal authority within the inner city. With their uniforms, guns, and cars, they present an image of power and control and are the most visible governmental response to specific incidents of violence. Police officers have daily encounters with children and families in crisis —

those involved in family violence, witnesses to crimes, or victims of aggression—and increasingly come in contact with children who are the perpetrators or victims of aggression.

At their best, traditional police strategies and tactics can provide children and families a sense of security and safety through rapid, authoritative, and effective responses at times of difficulty. All too often, however, children's contacts with police officers arouse fewer comforting feelings and more negative ones. In the psychological lives of inner-city children, the appearance of police officers in the context of situations of aggression makes them the objects for displacement of children's and families' rage. Their arrival "after the fact" strengthens children's view of society as unprotective; and the role of police as symbols of the dominant culture may shape children's views of them as representatives of an alien, uncaring outside world (Marans and Cohen, 1993; Marans, 1994). In fact, the contacts between police and children are affected by the fact that the child or parent may be a suspect or reluctant witness, and police officers—especially in the midst of a crisis—may not think about children's emotional needs. Negative encounters may further reinforce a child's view of society as uncaring and aggressive. These experiences may create and strengthen a child's belief that hostile behavior—being rough, tough, and bullying—is not only appropriate and reasonable in certain situations but is the normative mode of adult functioning. There are too few countervailing models of social authority available in an inner-city child's world.

## COMMUNITY MENTAL HEALTH

Like the police, mental health professionals involved with children and families have also begun to change the ways in which they deliver services by moving beyond the consulting room and joining forces with other professionals and community institutions.

In 1970 the Joint Commission on Mental Health of Children issued a landmark report that called attention to the inadequacies of the existing system of care for children with severe mental health disorders and urged the development of partnerships between parents, agencies, and institutions and federal, state, and local systems to meet the needs of these children and their families. In the intervening decades, there have been numerous national attempts to implement the recommendations of the Joint Commission: to create sustainable models of comprehensive care which break down the traditional boundaries between public and private agencies and institutions and to involve the entire community in identifying the children most in need of intervention and developing appropriate and responsive services.

The history of these efforts was unremarkable until 1983, when the National Institute of Mental Health created the Child and Adolescent Services System Program (CASSP), the progenitor of contemporary efforts to build integrated systems of care. The CASSP program, which attempts to synthesize the best previous efforts to encourage integrated service systems, has four major goals:

- creating interagency collaborations within each state which are able to address the complex needs of children with severe mental health disturbances;
- increasing capacity of the state agency responsible for children's services, including mental health, to provide appropriate care;
- expanding parental involvement in making decisions relevant to the care of children;
- developing a community-based, advocacy-oriented interdisciplinary planning process.

These goals take into account both prior federal and state experiences and the findings of Knitzer (1982), who documented the extent of children's unmet needs and urged traditional mental health providers to join with others who regularly serve children to address their multidimensional needs. As the negative effects of such familial stressors as disease, poverty, alcoholism, chemical dependency, violence, unemployment, inadequate housing, and lack of education became more widespread during the 1980s, new ways of intervening with children growing up in affected environments became essential. Programs and services focused on specific problems in the child's life had not proven effective.

The new paradigm for delivery of children's mental health services is centered in the child's community — his or her school, home, or neighborhood. In this model, provision of care is not limited to mental health professionals or constrained by the walls of the examining room. Others in the child's and family's world with whom they have ongoing relationships, including teachers, police officers, or coaches, may be the most appropriate intervenors. In this system the role of the mental health professional may be to screen, assess, refer, or provide direct clinical treatment, or it may be to act as consultant and backup for others who have developed important working alliances with the child and family. In short, the paradigmatic service system should be sufficiently flexible to allow for a case-by-case determination of the most appropriate mode of intervention and should be sufficiently integrated to facilitate access to the full range of public and private resources available in the community.

## A COLLABORATIVE RESPONSE TO URBAN VIOLENCE

The Child Development–Community Policing (CD-CP) Program developed out of the shared concerns of the leadership within the New Haven Department of Police Service and the Yale Child Study Center faculty. The program is a collaborative effort aimed at facilitating the response of mental health professionals and police to the burdens of violence on children, families, and the community. Through the application of the principles learned in work with schools and agencies (Comer, 1980; Comer and Haynes, 1990; Comer et al., 1991), the program attempts to change the atmosphere of police departments in relation to children and to increase the competence of police officers in their varied interactions with children and families. Fundamentally, the program attempts to reorient police officers in their interactions with children in order to optimize the psychological roles which they can play as providers of a sense of security, positive authority, and models for identification. In turn, through a reorientation of their traditional relationships with police professionals, the program aims to extend the roles that mental health clinicians play in the lives of children and families exposed to violence (Marans and Cohen, 1993; Marans, Berkman, and Cohen, in press).

The CD-CP program is closely related to and dependent upon the reorientation of the New Haven police toward a community-based policing philosophy, which focuses on early intervention and crime prevention rather than on incident response alone. The community-based policing philosophy provides officers with a conceptual framework to support their efforts on behalf of children. The practical strategy of placing individual officers on long-term assignment in particular neighborhoods provides officers with opportunities for developing relationships and assuming roles in children's lives that would not occur in a more impersonal, incident-driven policing system. The CD-CP program aims to provide the ongoing psychological training and operational support that officers need to make the best use of these new opportunities.

## PROGRAM COMPONENTS

The collaborative CD-CP program model consists of interrelated educational and clinical components that aim at sharing knowledge between police officers and clinicians.

### Child Development Fellowships

Community-based policing requires supervisors to be committed to the philosophy of neighborhood policing and prepared to translate the concepts into practice. The supervisors are responsible for all the work in their districts, set the tone of police work within the community, and serve as models for younger officers. Especially during the lengthy transition to community-based policing, supervisors face challenges in trying to implement goals in relation to early intervention, work with vulnerable children, youth, and families, and collaboration with other agencies. The Child Development Fellowship provides supervisory officers with special expertise in relation to these tasks.

Child development fellows are police supervisors who spend several hours a week over the course of several months in the collaborating mental health agency. With the guidance of a mentor from the clinical faculty, police fellows participate in a range of activities, similar to those of residents in psychiatry, which familiarize them with developmental concepts, patterns of psychological disturbance, methods of clinical intervention, and settings for treatment and care. Police supervisors involved in the fellowship also provide basic knowledge about police practice to their mental health colleagues. A major goal of the fellowship is to establish relationships between the fellows and the child mental health professionals with whom they will be collaborating in future.

### Police Fellowship for Clinical Faculty

Basic familiarity with the concerns and practices of police officers is essential for mental health professionals who intend to develop trusting collegial relationships with officers and explore collaborative intervention strategies. Through the fellowship program, clinicians spend time with police colleagues in squad cars, in police stations, and in the streets, observing officers' day-to-day activities. These experiences allow mental health professionals to familiarize themselves with police operations, local neighborhoods, and the realities of officers' interactions with children and families. The fellowship also provides opportunities for clinicians and officers to spend time together discussing their varied perspectives and approaches to serving youth and families and to explore ideas for new modes of collaboration.

### Education of Police Officers

In the past in the United States, the model police recruit was nineteen to twenty-two years old, had some experience in the military or with a security organization, and had a high school diploma or some college education. Increasingly, police officers are being recruited from inner-city and minority backgrounds, are somewhat older, and have a broader range of educational and professional experiences. However, there is no requirement that a recruit have any prior education in criminal justice or any training in basic principles of human functioning. Academic preparation for police work is provided at the police academy, where basic skills are acquired, and then in the field, where recruits receive supervised training. The education of police officers in most cities does not prepare them for much of the work in which they will be engaged, especially not the demands of community-based policing — dealing with the psychological impact of family violence, engaging with children and youth in situations of high risk, helping to divert possible offenders, collaborating in neighborhood improvement, and assisting those who have been the victims of crime.

The CD-CP seminar on child development, human functioning, and policing strategies aims at providing supervisors with both knowledge and a sense of personal empowerment to think about and help their officers intervene positively with children and families. The seminar meets weekly for ten weeks. Exposure to child development principles introduces officers to the importance of thinking about children's development and their own influence on children. Also, the course provides officers with the experience of working alongside mental health professionals and with concepts and methods for working cooperatively with other social services on behalf of children. The knowledge gained in this seminar improves the effectiveness, impact, and safety of police officers interacting with young people. It also enhances officers' self-image as positive role models within the community.

### Consultation Service

When an officer comes into contact with a child or youth in great danger or distress or becomes responsible for disposition, or action to be taken in the case, he or she must make an immediate decision whether to intervene and what is in the child's best interest (Goldstein, Freud, and Solnit, 1973, 1979; Goldstein et al., 1986). At times, intervention is clearly mandated, as when a child is determined to be the victim of abuse and the local child welfare agency must be notified. At other times, the critical nature of a medical condition (following an assault or a suicide attempt) dictates the involvement of emergency medical services. Yet officers frequently face situations in which there is no clearly mandated and available service. An officer who finds children who have witnessed an accident or assault, who has a teenager confide in him or her about being worried about gang membership, or who observes a child becoming truant is offered "clinical" opportunities for intervention which are broader than those usually considered the province of police work. It is within the officer's discretion as to how to proceed. As police officers work more closely with communities, these situations occur with greater frequency, and officers need a resource to turn to for discussion, guidance, and an immediate clinical response, especially when the child is in great distress, as happens so often in relation to inner-city violence.

The consultation service of the CD-CP program allows the police to make referrals and to have clinicians respond to officers' immediate needs for guidance, especially following children's traumatic experiences. Consultation service clinicians carry beepers and are on call twenty-four hours a day to discuss problems of children and youth with the police. At times, the consultation leads to referral to a clinical program, for example, the child psychiatric emergency service, a local child welfare agency, an outpatient mental health clinic, or mental health personnel within the child's school. However, at times a direct clinical response is needed because of the urgency of the child's distress. At such times, consultation service clinicians can respond immediately and see children and youth at the clinic, in the police station, or at the child's home.

### Program Conference

Police officers and clinicians who staff the CD-CP program meet weekly to discuss difficult and perplexing cases that arise from the officers' direct experience, as well as to plan and evaluate program activities and to integrate knowledge gained through the program. The program conference provides a regular forum for discussions aimed at maintaining the program's overall coherence and fostering the individual and institutional relationships on which the program is based.

In the conference, cases are discussed from many different points of view — in relation to the child and family's specific problems, the reasons for their interaction with the police, the types of services that they have used or may require, barriers to intervention, and specific problems posed to police officers and other agencies involved. The case discussions emphasize the importance of trying to understand the inner experience and meaning of events to children and adolescents; how psychological understanding can guide police and clinical work more effectively; the feelings aroused in the professionals by the children, families, or situations; and how the feelings of the professionals may interfere with or be used to inform intervention. The program conference also provides a forum for the discussion of systemic, institutional, and administrative issues.

### THE EXPERIENCE OF COLLABORATION

During the first three years of the CD-CP program's operation in New Haven, more than four hundred and fifty children were referred to the consultation service by officers in the field. The first calls, involving children exposed to some form of violence, were made by officers who had participated in the child development seminar or worked in neighborhoods supervised by the clinical fellows or by the supervisors themselves. A sample of these incidents follows.

A five-year-old girl was caught in the cross fire of a gang shooting and was struck by a .45 caliber bullet that lodged in her lower right jaw. She and her family were seen by a psychotherapist from the moment she entered the hospital and after she was discharged.

A twelve-year-old girl ran away from home when her mother and the mother's boyfriend began fighting at home. When the girl was five years old, a similar situation had developed between her parents and ended with the mother shooting her father after he beat her repeatedly. The girl and mother were referred for psychotherapy, for the first time, by neighborhood police officers. When the mother ended her relationship with the abusive boyfriend, the police remained in close contact with the family and negotiated and

supervised the boyfriend's move out of the home. The girl
then returned home.

A thirteen-year-old girl was charged with murdering her
newborn infant. The girl and her mother were referred for
evaluation and treatment by the investigating police officers.

A sixteen-year-old gang member was referred by the police
after suffering a full-blown panic attack while being ar-
raigned for the shooting death of a close friend. Despite his
having spent two years in a correctional facility, this was the
first time the boy had been evaluated by mental health professionals.

A fifteen-year-old girl was seen in the hospital and for
follow-up consultations after she was shot in the chest and
arm while sitting in a car with three friends. The shooting
was apparently drug related. Her best friend died as a result
of the shooting, and another companion suffered serious
neurological damage as a result of his wounds.

Prior to the institution of the Child Development–Community Policing Program, officers probably would have not taken
notice of the psychological distress these children suffered; if they
noticed, it would have been unlikely that they had knowledge of or
access to appropriate mental health services to meet the children's
needs. These children and many others like them probably would
not have come to the attention of the mental health or social service systems until they experienced serious behavioral disturbances
months or years later.

With the cases seen through the consultation service, clinicians and police officers in New Haven are learning about the
impact of inner-city violence on children and their families. Working together, they are developing strategies for both the consulting

room and the streets for interrupting and minimizing the effects of that violence. In addition, the relationship forged between clinicians and police has generated a broader understanding of the needs of inner-city youth and ideas about how best to serve them.

This manual outlines the components of the Child Development–Community Policing Program. Although individual communities may vary enormously in terms of available resources, the manual attempts to convey a framework for mental health and police collaboration. For too long these professionals have operated independently in pursuit of similar interests and concerns. Now mental health clinicians and police are collaborating to minimize the effects of violence and interrupt the cycle of destructive and antisocial behavior. When these professionals begin to discuss common challenges and act in tandem, they do so on behalf of children and families who are most vulnerable to violence in the community.

MIRIAM BERKMAN
DOUGLAS MACDONALD
STEVEN MARANS
STEVEN NAGLER
MELVIN WEARING

# 2 Child Development Fellowships

A child development fellowship provides selected supervisory police officers with an extended period of training and consultation with mental health professionals and an introduction to available programs for the evaluation and treatment of children and families. The basic clinical content of the fellowship includes material similar to the CD-CP seminar, however, the experiential and collaborative format of the fellowship facilitates the development of working relationships between officers and clinicians and provides police supervisors with additional tools for leading other officers. Simultaneously, the fellowship exposes a selected group of clinicians to the daily activities and concerns of police professionals.

The fellowship has four primary goals:

- to provide leaders in the police force with the psychological expertise they need to guide other officers in a variety of crime prevention, early intervention, and relationship-building activities involving children, adolescents, families, and community agencies;
- to develop a group of specially trained, respected veteran officers who can disseminate the CD-CP program's philosophy and methods within the police department through their relationships with other officers;
- to provide the mental health professionals most involved in the CD-CP collaboration with the basic knowledge of police practices they need to work effectively with their police colleagues; and
- to develop close, trusting working relationships between police supervisors and clinicians which facilitate the training and consultative elements of the CD-CP program.

The fellowship program permits supervisory officers and clinical faculty to establish basic knowledge, respect for each other's work, a core of common experience, and a shared frame of reference. This shared exposure, teaching, and learning encourages ongoing, trusting relationships between officers and mental health professionals. The CD-CP program depends on these relationships to support collaboration in response to specific crises referred to the consultation service and in developing the CD-CP program, as well as increasing interest in collaboration among other officers and clinicians, through both training and informal contact.

Child development fellows are supervisory police officers who spend several hours a week for ten weeks in the cooperating mental health setting. During the fellowship, they are exposed to a range of clinical activities, including clinical case conferences and observations of clinical evaluations, in order to become familiar with developmental concepts, patterns of psychological disturbance, methods of clinical intervention, and settings for care and treatment. The knowledge these officers gain regarding development and human behavior, family relations, and available mental health services is applied in their work as police officers and as supervisors. Basic familiarity with psychological concepts and approaches of mental health service also allows officers to become active partners with mental health professionals in formulating collaborative interventions for children and families who are unlikely to benefit from traditional law enforcement or mental health approaches applied in isolation.

Collaboration can take different forms. In one scenario, a sergeant just beginning the fellowship was called to the scene of a fatal stabbing. After the incident he was disturbed by recurring thoughts of a girl whom the police had told to wait on the porch alone while they interviewed adults in the house. After presenting the case for discussion with clinicians and other officers, the sergeant went back to the house and offered the family a referral to the consultation service. The case also stimulated a more general discussion among officers and clinicians about how to balance children's need — for the consistent presence of familiar adults at times of stress and trauma and their need to be shielded from gory scenes of violence — and officers' need — to conduct prompt investigative interviews with parents who are witnesses to crimes. Officers suggested a variety of alternatives, including designating a family member or a police officer to stay with the child, away from the immediate scene of violence.

During the course of the fellowship, police supervisors visit the local juvenile detention facility, which can also open new avenues of communication. Although the officers are familiar with some of the institution's residents, this is usually the first time that they have seen the reformatory. After a tour, officers listen while a clinical faculty member interviews a resident about the youth's life and the youth's understanding of the pathways leading to his or her delinquent behavior, the experience of incarceration, and what it would take for the youth to avoid further criminal activity. Such interviews often reveal poignant histories of abuse, neglect, parental loss, academic and social failure, and hopelessness for the future, as well as repeated and escalating criminal activity. Officers thus confront the complexity of these teens' internal experience, the inaccuracy of categorical concepts of "victim" and "perpetrator," and the need for creative thinking regarding approaches to both treatment and law enforcement for this population. Following these visits, officers have proposed community-based collaborations among police officers, probation officers, and mental health clinicians to combine structure, external control, and clinical interventions in efforts to decrease juvenile crime in the community.

Officers participate in the program in small groups (four to six members) so that each fellow can develop personal relationships with clinicians. After they have completed the fellowship training, fellows remain involved in the CD-CP program as members of the program conference, as trainers of rank-and-file officers, and as members of the consultation service.

The police fellows also bring to the CD-CP program a broad range of experience that they use to teach their mental health colleagues about the realities of police work. These include risks to personal safety, burdens of exposure to multiple traumatic events, development of relationships with the full range of community members (including criminals), and frustrations associated with immersion in the daily lives of impoverished inner-city residents.

In addition, clinicians have an opportunity to see officers' refined skills of observation, their understanding of people with whom they come in contact, and the various productive uses of authority with community members who call for assistance as well as with those who participate in criminal activity. These phenomena are especially apparent when clinicians ride with officers on patrol. Extended contact with officers can also help clinicians expand their understanding of the day-to-day lives of the children and families the clinicians often see in isolated clinical settings. Basic familiarity with the concerns and practices of police officers is essential for mental health professionals to develop trusting, collegial relationships with officers and allows clinicians to think realistically about collaborative intervention strategies. Clinicians who have developed personal relationships within the police department and are familiar with police operations are also able to spread this knowledge within the collaborating mental health institution.

In an example of the value of observing police officers at work, a clinician and a sergeant spent an evening shift together responding to a series of calls regarding domestic disputes. The last call of the evening came from a twenty-three-year-old woman who had been beaten by her boyfriend. She screamed a litany of obscenities and revenge fantasies at the officers who took her complaint, while two young children anxiously clung to her side. When the sergeant, one of the first CD-CP fellows, commented about how upsetting the violence was for the children, the mother stopped screaming and began to talk about her four-year-old son's fears, nightmares, and aggressive behavior. The mother accepted the clinician's offer of a follow-up visit to discuss the child's experience and needs and then suggested that she was about to leave her children to go to a bar. As the sergeant and the clinician drove away, the sergeant observed the clinician staring out the window and commented, "It's the volume. You see some of these people in your office. Maybe you see them once a week. You know a lot about what makes them tick, maybe, but you only see them a little bit at a time. It's different out here. We see those kids all the time . . . and there's been nothing we could do."

The ride-along can provide a rare perspective on police work. A senior clinician spent an evening shift with an officer who had ten years' experience in a wide range of police work, including community patrol and undercover operations. As they rode from job to job, often more than one police car responded to a call. On several occasions, after completing their investigation, the officers spent a few minutes talking among themselves. The clinician's guide would then introduce him to the others. In general, officers expressed faint, if any, interest in the clinician's presence; he was essentially invisible. At one point in the evening, the officer pulled into a parking lot to write up a report. After a few minutes, she looked up and said, "I just realized that here I am writing this report and somebody who doesn't like cops could walk up to the car, put a gun to my head, and pull the trigger. The only people who know that feeling are cops." The clinician then understood his experience of invisibility in the context of the officers' shared sense of unique vulnerability.

## SELECTION OF PARTICIPANTS

The police supervisors and mental health professionals who participate in the fellowship constitute the core group who will be responsible for developing and maintaining interagency collaboration, training rank-and-file officers, and staffing the consultation service. Ideally, both the police fellows and core clinicians should be leaders in their own institutions and creative collaborators across disciplines, and should be committed to the development of the CD-CP program.

### Police Fellows

Broad representation of all sectors of the police department within the fellowship is essential. Criteria for selecting police fellows should include:

- leadership roles within the department;
- assignment to specialized positions involving children and families;
- interest in and commitment to addressing the needs of children through policing activities;
- personal strength as leaders of other officers; and
- interest and experience in interagency and interdisciplinary collaboration and institutional change.

In New Haven, for example, a majority of fellows have been community-based sergeants and lieutenants who are responsible for supervising district substations. It has been important to include other leadership positions: assistant chief of police, shift commanders, head of juvenile services unit, head of family violence and sex bias unit, and head of narcotics unit. From these leadership positions, the police fellows are able to spread the knowledge they gain in the fellowship training to rank-and-file officers under their supervision and introduce other officers to the personal relationships they have formed with the clinicians involved in the program.

Selection of the police fellows may be based on assignment by the chief and/or requests to participate. Whatever selection process is used, it is important to the acceptance of the fellows by their colleagues for the chief to articulate at the outset of the program a rationale for inclusion and a schedule for rotating the selected participants through the training and to distribute within the department a roster of those supervisors in key positions who will be included in the fellowship training.

### Mental Health Professionals

Selection of a core group of clinicians who are committed to developing and staffing the CD-CP program is also essential. Unlike the police fellows, who join an expanding core group with waves of three or four new fellows every four to six months, the core group of mental health professionals remains relatively constant, with expansion of clinical staffing determined by growth of the program and expanding demands for service. The difference in CD-CP staffing reflects the disparity in size between most police departments and mental health agencies: the greater numbers and multiple shifts within the police force requires a larger number of CD-CP fellows to disseminate the program's approach within the department.

Criteria for selecting the core clinical group should include:

- experience in clinical assessment and psychotherapy with children, adolescents, parents, and families, including those exposed to violence and other traumatic situations;
- experience and interest in modes of clinical intervention based at home, at school, and/or in the community;
- experience and interest in interdisciplinary and interagency collaborations and institutional change;
- leadership roles within the participating mental health agency;
- familiarity with mental health and social service resources in the community; and
- willingness to participate in a twenty-four-hour, on-call service.

Selection of the clinicians involved in the program may be based on assignment or request. For the program to have credibility within the mental health agency, the clinicians must have the active support of the agency director.

**FELLOWSHIP TRAINING**

## Familiarizing Police Officers with Mental Health Concepts and Activities

The mental health resources available to serve children and families vary from community to community, and the specific content of a child development fellowship will therefore depend on the general resources available and the strengths of the participating local mental health institution. In most communities, the mental health institution that provides the most comprehensive range of services to children and families is likely to be in the best position to provide police officers with exposure to the most varied clinical services as well as full discussion of the psychological concepts underlying those services. The officer training component of the fellowship has two central elements, clinical rotations for observation and post-observation discussions.

*Clinical Rotations for Observation*  Officers are exposed to observations and discussions of a wide range of mental health services for children and families, including outpatient evaluations, emergency room services, juvenile delinquency institutions, and case conferences regarding home- and clinic-based treatments. Officers in the fellowship may also view videotaped materials as in the CD-CP seminars. These direct observations allow officers and clinicians to share their common skills of careful observation and drawing inferences from small behavioral details. The rotations for observation and discussion are coordinated for each group of fellows, with some rotations attended by officers individually and others by the entire group. The rotations expose officers to the day-to-day work of the clinicians with whom they will be working and to useful ways of thinking about and understanding human behavior. (See figure 2.1 for a schedule from the New Haven fellowship.)

Figure 2.1. Sample Schedule from the New Haven Child Development-Community Policing Fellowship

| Week | Day | Time | Session | Comments |
|------|-----|------|---------|----------|
| 1 | Wednesday | 9:45–11:00 | Program conference | CD-CP weekly meeting |
|   | Thursday | 10:30–12:00 | Child development | Introductory discussion |
| 2 | Wednesday | 9:45–11:00 | Program conference | |
|   | Thursday | 10:30–12:00 | *John* | Film and discussion |
| 3 | Monday | 10:30–11:30 | Outpatient clinic | Introduction to clinic |
|   | Wednesday | 9:45–11:00 | Program conference | |
| 4 | Monday | 11:30–1:00 | Outpatient clinic | Observe team meeting |
|   | Wednesday | 9:45–11:00 | Program conference | |
| 5 | Wednesday | 9:45–11:00 | Program conference | |
|   | Thursday | 8:30–10:00 | Home-based services | Team meeting with child welfare |
| 6 | Wednesday | 9:45–11:00 | Program conference | |
|   | Thursday | 10:15–11:45 | Outpatient clinic | Observe evaluation interview |
| 7 | Wednesday | 9:45–11:00 | Program conference | |
|   | Thursday | 10:15–11:45 | Outpatient clinic | Observe evaluation interview |
| 8 | Wednesday | 9:45–11:00 | Program conference | |
|   | Thursday | 10:15–11:45 | Outpatient clinic | Observe evaluation interview |
| 9 | Wednesday | 9:45–11:00 | Program conference | |
|   | Thursday | 10:15–11:45 | Outpatient clinic | Observe evaluation interview |
| 10 | Wednesday | 9:45–11:00 | Program conference | |
|   | Thursday | 9:00–11:30 | Juvenile reformatory | Tour — no uniform |
| 11 | Wednesday | 9:45–11:00 | Program conference | |
|   | Wednesday | 11:10–12:00 | Case consultation with CD-CP faculty | |
| 12 | Monday | 9:00–11:00 | School | Tour / discussion |
|   | Wednesday | 9:45–11:00 | Program conference | |
| 13 | Wednesday | 9:45–11:00 | Program conference | |
|   | Wednesday | 11:10–12:00 | Case consultation with CD-CP faculty | |
| 14 | Tuesday | 1:30–3:00 | Hospital emergency room and pediatric ward | Tour / discussion (2 fellows) |
|   | Wednesday | 9:45–11:00 | Program conference | |

| Week | Day | Time | Session | Comments |
|------|-----|------|---------|----------|
| 15 | Tuesday | 1:30–3:00 | Hospital emergency room and pediatric ward | Tour/discussion (2 fellows) |
| | Wednesday | 9:45–11:00 | Program conference | |
| 16 | Wednesday | 9:45–11:00 | Program conference | |
| | Wednesday | 11:10–12:00 | Case consultation with CD-CP faculty | |
| 17 | Wednesday | 9:45–11:00 | Program conference | |
| | Friday | 10:00–11:30 | Inpatient psychiatric unit | Tour/discussion — no uniform (2 fellows) |
| 18 | Wednesday | 9:45–11:00 | Program conference | |
| | Friday | 10:00–11:30 | Inpatient psychiatric unit | Tour/discussion — no uniform (2 fellows) |
| 19 | Wednesday | 9:45–11:00 | Program conference | |
| | Wednesday | 11:10–12:00 | Case consultation with CD-CP faculty | |
| 20 | Wednesday | 9:45–11:00 | Program conference | |
| | Wednesday | 11:10–12:00 | Case consultation with CD-CP faculty | |

*Note:* Not all rotations will be available in all communities, and other rotations may be added depending on available local resources.

A description of the rotations, along with their intended goals and effects, follows.

- *Outpatient clinic.* Observation and discussion of an outpatient evaluation exposes officers to a clinical approach to understanding a child or adolescent's problematic behavior and to clinical techniques for interacting with children and parents. This rotation gives officers firsthand knowledge of what a child and family are likely to experience in a clinical setting.
- *Home-based clinical services or Family Preservation Program case conferences.* Exposure of officers to discussions of cases served by intensive home-based clinical services provides a

sense of the clinical complexity of the families the officers encounter every day and introduces the types of clinical intervention that can be accomplished in very difficult families without removing children from their homes.

- *Juvenile reformatory.* Touring an institution for adjudicated juvenile delinquents shows officers the setting in which delinquents are confined and the limitations of the treatment offered there. Because of traditional boundaries between police departments and the juvenile justice system, many officers will never have seen this facility.
- *Public schools.* Exposure of officers to local public schools and their personnel encourages the development of good working relationships between police and school professionals. The rotation also familiarizes officers with the sorts of problems children may exhibit at school and some of the ways that school personnel can intervene.
- *Local hospital/consultation and liaison service.* Exposure of officers to the environment of the hospital, including emergency room and pediatric wards, provides a forum for discussing children's reactions to trauma and to hospitalization, stimulates officers' thinking about their interactions with hospital staff in emergency and investigative situations, and introduces them to some of the hospital personnel with whom they will collaborate in the future.
- *Psychiatric inpatient service.* The inpatient rotation exposes officers to children with the most severe psychiatric and behavioral disturbances in a carefully controlled treatment setting and provides a forum for discussion of some of the psychological bases of violent behavior.

*Post-Observation Discussions*  In post-observation discussions, the group of clinicians designated as collaborators from the participating mental health institution meets regularly with the fellows to discuss the underlying psychological principles that inform the various clinical services, questions and ideas that arise in response to the officers' observations, integration of officers' observations into a developmental framework, and the application of developmental principles to policing strategies. The regularity of the meetings and steady attendance by all participants promote continuity, an atmosphere supportive of inquiry, and the development of honest working relationships.

### Familiarizing Clinicians with Police Concepts and Activities

The clinician training component of the fellowship allows clinical faculty to familiarize themselves with police operations, local neighborhoods, and the day-to-day experiences of officers in the community, including issues of safety for officers and community members, uses of police authority, and the range of community response to police activity. These experiences provide opportunities for officers and clinicians to discuss their perspectives and approaches to serving youth and families in the city and to explore ideas for new modes of collaboration. As in the case of officers' training, the specific content of the clinicians' training will vary from community to community, depending on the organization of the local police department, the assignments of the central police collaborators, and the issues of most concern to the police and mental health participants in the program.

The fellowship training for clinicians has two main elements: regular ride-alongs, and observation and consultation in other police settings.

On ride-alongs, the clinician rides with the officer on a regular shift and observes while the officer responds to calls for assistance, has casual encounters with neighborhood residents, including children and adolescents, and collaborates with other officers.

Clinicians riding with officers observe police responses to a variety of situations, including domestic disputes, other assaults, burglaries, calls regarding shots fired, street interdiction of narcotics, and so on. Children may be present at any of these scenes, and officers' responses to children and parents offer valuable opportunities for discussion and collaboration. Discussion before and during ride-alongs also teach clinicians about the risks officers face and the precautions they can take to ensure their safety.

The ride-alongs should take place in a variety of neighborhoods and on all shifts to allow clinicians to become familiar with the diversity of the police department's work and to become visible to a greater number of rank-and-file officers. Although clinicians may ride with supervisors or other officers who are not part of the fellowship program in order to see neighborhoods or shifts that are not represented within the core group of police collaborators, ride-alongs with supervisors within the fellowship group ordinarily offer more opportunities to build on the relationships developed in the other components of the fellowship training. When clinicians ride with officers outside the fellowship, it is important that a police fellow introduces the clinician to his or her fellow officers so that clinicians may more readily be perceived as colleagues.

In addition to ride-alongs, clinicians spend time with police supervisors observing the activities of neighborhood police teams and specialty units, including juvenile services, family violence, and narcotics. For example, a clinician who spends a shift with the head of a narcotics unit gets a much clearer understanding of the daily operations of street-level drug activity as well as various policing intervention strategies. A clinician who spends a shift with the head of a domestic violence unit participates in discussions among detectives regarding patterns of escalating violence, options for enhanced prosecutions, the impact of ongoing violence on children in the family, and officers' frustration when victims of violence return repeatedly to violent relationships. Clinicians' presence in police stations, substations, and specialty units allows them to learn more about the work of officers, build relationships that will facilitate future collaboration, and participate in case conferences or informal consultations regarding situations in which officers come in contact with children and families in trouble or in which police activities may have a psychological impact on children.

## ISSUES RAISED BY THE FELLOWSHIP COLLABORATION

The child development fellowship program creates new roles for police officers as participant-observers in clinical settings and for mental health professionals as participant-observers in police settings. As in any form of collaboration, involvement in another profession's domain raises inevitable concerns regarding potential disruptions of established routines and scrutiny. When police and mental health professionals collaborate, other issues may arise. As examples, some conflicts that arose in New Haven and their resolutions are discussed below. Similar issues may be resolved in different ways in other communities, depending on law, professional norms, and personal preferences, by the relevant collaborators as part of their work together.

### Confidentiality

During the child development fellowship, officers observe clinical evaluations and conferences regarding children and families whose identities become known to the police fellows. In addition to the general concern common to all clinical teaching programs about disclosing such confidential clinical data to individuals not directly involved in a patient's care, police participation in these activities poses a unique potential for conflict between officers' sworn duty to enforce the law and their duty as members of an interdisciplinary clinical team not to disclose confidential clinical information. In order to protect the subjects of discussion from inappropriate and unwanted clinical disclosure and the officers from any charge that they have failed to uphold their police duty, some of the following measures can be useful.

- Any patients whose evaluations are observed directly by the police fellows must give informed consent. Patients should be informed that observers will not interrupt the interviews in any way and, if possible, that observers will be out of view behind a mirror. Where possible, patients selected for observation should live outside the jurisdiction of the participating police department so that officers will be less likely to know the individuals observed.
- When clinical material is presented in a conference in order to illustrate principles of human development, clinicians are advised to remove any identifying information from their accounts or to present hypothetical or composite examples.
- Officers participating in the fellowship may sign waivers stating that information concerning specific individuals learned in the course of fellowship activities will be kept confidential and will not be used as the basis of any police action, unless independently reported pursuant to state mandate. (See figure 2.2 for a copy of the waiver form used in New Haven.)
- Officers should absent themselves from any clinical discussion if they are aware that the subject of discussion is also the subject of a criminal investigation. Although it is extremely unlikely that information about a patient presented in a clinical case conference will be relevant to a police investigation, the only way to protect the patient's confidentiality is to exclude the officers from the discussion.

Figure 2.2. Sample Waiver Form

I, _____, understand that my participation in the Child Study Center-New Haven Police Department Clinical Fellowship program requires that any and all information learned about patients or individuals seeking consultation and/or other clinical services, as well as any and all information learned incidentally about any other person in the course of my participation in the Clinical Fellowship program, will be regarded by me as confidential; such information will not be communicated by me to any other person on or off the New Haven Police Force, and will not form the basis of any arrest or criminal investigation or be used in any other aspect of police work.

Signed: _____

Date: _____

---

- Clinicians may find that their exposure to information about a patient, without the patient's knowledge, in the context of discussions or conferences with police officers, makes it difficult for the clinician to maintain a sense of therapeutic neutrality in relation to the patient. In such cases the clinician should absent himself or herself from any discussions with the police about the patient. (See chapter 4 for further discussion.)

These guidelines provide helpful starting points for addressing many dilemmas regarding confidentiality and professional boundaries. Especially at the beginning of the collaboration, careful attention to issues of confidentiality allows professionals of different disciplines to explore their common interests and learn from each other without jeopardizing their own professional values and identities; it also increases the likelihood of support for the collaboration from members of both institutions who are not directly involved in the program. Ongoing and open discussions about these issues are an essential part of developing an enduring collaboration between mental health and police professionals.

### Clinicians' Participation in Police Activities

The CD-CP program familiarizes mental health professionals with the basic workings of a police department by placing clinicians in police cars, community substations, and other neighborhood settings. Clinicians' presence in these environments presents challenges regarding possible danger and civil liability. These issues can be addressed in several ways, both formal and informal.

Some concerns regarding danger and disruption can be addressed individually between officers and clinicians. In New Haven, for example, officers have taken the lead in showing their mental health colleagues a wide range of their work, including routine patrols, narcotics raids, and hostage negotiations. Clinicians have not been invited into situations in which the officer felt the clinician would be in danger or would be in the way — for instance, clinicians waited in the car until the premises were secure before entering an apartment that was the subject of a search warrant.

Clinicians riding with police officers may be required to sign waivers of liability assuming the risk of any injury that might occur to the civilian clinician during his or her presence with the police. Lawyers for the city and the participating mental health agency may be consulted in drafting and approving any such waiver. (See figure 2.3 for a copy of the form used in New Haven.)

Clinicians may be required to obtain permission for each ride-along or other observation from the chief of police or his designee so that the potential for danger and disruption is minimized and tightly controlled at the highest levels of the police administration. However, this option places obstacles in the way of spontaneous, independent collaboration between officers and clinicians and may inhibit the development of open, collegial relationships.

# DEPARTMENT OF POLICE SERVICE

*One Union Ave, New Haven CT 06519*

*Nicholas Pastore*
*Chief of Police*

*John DeStefano, Jr.*
*Mayor*

Mr./Mrs./Ms._____has my permission to ride

as an observer with a _____unit

on _____from_____to_____.
        (date)         (hours)        (hours)

This slip will be retained by the Division Supervisor, effected,

and attached to Waiver slip signed by the above.  No permission

to ride in vehicles will be allowed beyond the dates and hours

stated above.

*Nicholas Pastore*

NICHOLAS PASTORE
CHIEF OF POLICE

-----------------------------------------------------------------

## W A I V E R

TO BE EXECUTED BY EACH SWORN OR CIVILIAN OBSERVER ASSIGNED TO
ACCOMPANY POLICE PERSONNEL.  THE WAIVER FORM IS TO BE FILLED OUT
PRIOR TO EACH ASSIGNMENT, REGARDLESS OF WHETHER PRIOR WAIVERS
HAVE BEEN EXECUTED.

I, _____, VOLUNTARILY AND WILLINGLY
ASSUME ALL RISKS INCIDENT TO ACCOMPANYING A NEW HAVEN POLICE
OFFICER IN THE PERFORMANCE OF HIS/HER DUTIES.  DURING SUCH
ACCOMPANIMENT, I SHALL ACT ONLY AS AN OBSERVER.

_____    _____
(NAME)                  (ADDRESS)

_____    _____
(ORGANIZATION)         (CITY/STATE)

TO BE NOTARIZED BY DESK OFFICER

SUBSCRIBED AND SWORN TO BEFORE ME THIS_____DAY OF_____,

19_____.

*Pride & Progress*

Figure 2.3. New Haven Department of Police Service Waiver Form

Clinicians may be designated as civilian consultants to the police department and provided with appropriate identification cards entitling them to be present at scenes of police activity. By limiting the identification cards to the core group of clinicians staffing the CD-CP program, the police department may sufficiently control civilian observation without requiring day-by-day authorization from the chief for each ride-along by a mental health professional.

### Guns and Uniforms in a Clinical Setting

Police officers in uniform carrying guns, nightsticks, handcuffs, and other equipment graphically represent power and physical strength in the hands of societal authority. Concerns are common among mental health professionals that the presence of uniformed officers in the halls and conference rooms of the child mental health clinics may frighten and alienate patients. Clinicians worry that children can be made anxious by the officers' presence and, by association, feel unsafe in the clinic where they come for treatment. Similarly, clinicians may worry that parents, some of whom have previous or current criminal involvement that did not involve their children, might withdraw their children from care rather than maintain alliances with professionals who were now identified with the police.

Traditionally, police have entered child mental health facilities only in response to crises or criminal activity. The CD-CP program provides an opportunity for officers to be seen by clinicians and patients alike as positive figures of benign authority and as agents of service. For this opportunity to be realized, it is crucial for the police and mental health collaborators to be centrally involved in developing the program and to be sensitive to the issues raised by the presence of uniformed officers in clinical settings. Officers, the core group of clinicians in the CD-CP program, and other clinicians from the collaborating mental health agency should have opportunities to discuss the psychological implications for children, parents, and mental health professionals of regular exposure to uniformed officers in the mental health setting. Officers may also be required to attend some clinical rotations during the fellowship unarmed and in street clothes. For example, seriously disturbed or psychotic children on a psychiatric inpatient unit may not be able to understand that uniformed officers are present on the unit to observe and not to punish the child's "bad" thoughts or deeds.

In general, the observations and discussions that make up the fellowship program provide supervisory officers and clinicians with a forum and a process to develop both an understanding of one another's work and the collegial relationships that will facilitate collaboration between their respective institutions. Especially in the early stages of the program's implementation, the fellowship — together with the experience of the first cases referred through the consultation service — set the tone for developing the open working relationships, including the resolution of inevitable interdisciplinary tensions, on which the program's success depends.

STEVEN NAGLER
STEVEN MARANS
MIRIAM BERKMAN

# 3  Training Seminars

The Child Development–Community Policing training seminars are intended to introduce police officers to the basic principles of child development and human behavior as useful tools of daily police work. The seminars capitalize on police officers' well-developed observation skills, aiming to expand an officer's field of observation to include child and adolescent behavior, as well as parent-child interactions. The practical nature of the seminar subject is emphasized through the use of field-based scenarios and the experiences of the seminar participants. Although the seminars proceed according to developmental sequence, each discussion attempts to link the inner life of the child and manifest behaviors seen at the original phase of development with the ways in which these phenomena may be observed in various forms throughout the life cycle.

Throughout the seminars it is crucial that the leaders convey the notion that a greater understanding of human functioning does not mean inaction, decreased vigilance with regard to issues of personal safety, or simply feeling sympathetic toward any and all subjects of their interventions. The goal of the seminars is to demonstrate the ways in which officers' consideration of principles of development and human functioning can enhance the range of strategies for dealing with various situations and can help establish a realistic appreciation of the potential impact they can have on the lives of children and families with whom they interact.

Training seminars are led by a team comprised of a clinical faculty member and a supervisory police officer who has completed the child development fellowship. This team provides credibility of course content and police experience. The working relationship between instructors is an important model of police-clinician collaboration. Instructors are encouraged to spend some time working together in the field and preparing the course in order to develop a comfortable, mutually respectful partnership.

Seminar groups are kept small (twelve to fifteen officers) in order to foster informal discussion in sessions that generally run for ninety minutes each. It is a good idea to open each session by asking whether anyone has had a situation or a case which bears on the topics last discussed. This gives the instructors and class members the opportunity to apply the principles and ideas of the seminar directly. Instructors are encouraged to use experiences from their work and from their own lives. Officers may be reluctant to be more personal or to disclose more than the instructors, so the instructors must set the tone.

The seminar has three main aims in preparation of officers. *Awareness of the principles of child and family development in order to understand and appreciate the effects of violence and other situations on children and to make appropriate referrals to the consultation service.* For example, a woman on her way to the laundromat with her five-year-old daughter is robbed at gunpoint in front of her home. In addition to taking the information about the crime, an officer asks the mother about her daughter's reaction and offers a referral to the consultation service if the mother wishes.

*Use of the principles of child and adolescent development to better inform their field judgment as they deal with children and adolescents in their daily routine.* For example, after being called to the scene of a fight between two teenaged girls in front of a large group of their peers on a street corner, responding officers separate the young women from each other and from the crowd in order to diminish the effects of the peer group.

*Understanding of their own reactions and counterreactions to anxiety, stress, and frustration as these affect their performance.* For example, a nineteen-year-old mother of two children under three years old swears at an officer who is responding to a complaint that the children have been left alone in the dark and messy apartment. The officer is able to bear in mind his or her own frustration at the situation of the children and the mother's defensive reaction to any authority and persists in an attempt to engage the mother in a conversation which can result in a referral to the consultation service.

**SEMINAR OUTLINE**

Week 1.  Introduction. Rationale for course, relationship to police work, introduction to psychological concepts

Week 2.  Infancy: Birth to Three Years. Basic needs of children; the central role of the parent

Week 3.  Separation and Trauma: Eighteen Months to Three Years. The effects of separation on young children

Week 4. Young Children: Four to Six Years. Observations
and case presentations

Week 5. School-Age Children: Seven to Eleven Years.
Observations and case presentations

Week 6. Puberty and Early Adolescence. Developmental
challenges and symptomatology

Week 7. Issues of Race and Socioeconomic Status in Child
Development and Community Policing

Week 8. Adolescence. Developmental challenges and
symptomatology

Week 9. Conclusion. Community mental health resources
and course evaluation

### Notes to Instructors

The session-by-session outlines that follow are intended as a
guide to course development for the instructor teams who lead the
course. They are designed to give some direction to those who are
leading this course for the first time and are not intended to replace
the experience, training, and judgment of the instructor teams.
The officers and clinicians in each locality that implements this
series of seminars will have different backgrounds, experience, and
training. For this seminar to be successful, it must be tailored to the
situation in which it is presented. In addition to the practical neces-
sity for site-by-site course development, the process of working
together on the course, we have found, has been rewarding, en-
lightening, and fun for the instructor teams.

The scenarios that accompany the session outlines are taken
from the experience of officers and clinicians in the New Haven
Child Development–Community Policing Program. They are intended as examples of the kind of scenarios that have been used
in teaching situations. Instructors are encouraged to develop scenarios from their own experiences — a profitable exercise for new
instructors to learn with and about each other. Specifically devel-

oped scenarios have more detail and local color, which enhance their usefulness.

### 1. INTRODUCTION

#### Key Concepts

- The course is about a way of seeing and thinking, not about learning a specific body of child development knowledge. Success in this course will be measured by officers' ability to ask the right questions, not by their ability to give the right answers.
- The world looks different through the eyes of a child. Officers will be asked to consider the perspective of children throughout the course.
- Child, adolescent, and adult behavior has roots in developmental struggles and tasks, as well as in reason, logic, obedience, and morality. All these considerations are important tools for officers as they attempt to respond safely and authoritatively in their work. Behavior that seems to defy logic may reflect an individual's experiences of threat and/or danger and the individual's attempts to deal with those experiences. Internal and external distress (which may revive memory of past distress) may reverse development or throw it off the expected course. These problematic responses will look different at each developmental phase, depending on the individual child's strengths, weaknesses, family, environment, and so on.

#### Process

Although this first session has the least content as such, in many ways it is the most important of the series. The co-leaders must create an atmosphere of seriousness of purpose, confidentiality (what is said here stays here), usefulness to police work, and openness. The session should be held in a seminar setting with officers and instructors seated around a table or in a circle. A formal classroom setting with instructors in front of a class is not recommended. It is important to emphasize the issues of confidentiality and the lack of right and wrong answers. This will set the stage for the entire course and will set it apart from other, more formal types of training situations with which officers will be familiar. Each officer should be invited to introduce himself or herself. Introductions should include siblings, children, previous or current involvement with children, and any thoughts they have about the course or their work with children as police officers. This task should take up most of the session. Instructors can comment on the officers' stories and draw individuals out. By doing so, they set the conversational and informal tone for the rest of the course.

### 2. INFANCY: BIRTH TO THREE YEARS

#### Key Concepts

- Attachment is a crucial concept in the development of children. Reliability and consistency in those who care for a child form the basis of a secure attachment. This is the cornerstone of developmental progress and of the capacity to deal with stress and trauma. When the primary attachments to caregivers are disrupted significantly, the child may be overwhelmed and unable to cope with normal developmental tasks and stress, as well as with situations of trauma.
- Infants need protection and nurturing. They are unable to care for themselves.
- Infants have limited ability to cope with stress and trauma. The main capacity an infant has to respond to any situation

of stress is to cry and thereby signal his or her need for help or to withdraw into lethargy and/or sleep if repeated crying is ignored. Infants who are overwhelmed may exhibit disturbances of sleeping or eating and the inability to be soothed due to their limited capacity to cope with stress.

- The importance of the mother- or caretaker-infant relationship. The mother's ability to "read" the infant and anticipate and/or react to the infant's needs is central to the infant's physical and emotional development. The mother, therefore, needs to be protected and nurtured as part of the mother-infant unit.

- The infant has an inner world and is more than a passive acceptor of care. The infant has perceptions and experiences of physical and emotional states which are highly significant to future development. These occur primarily within the mother-child relationship.

### Process

The session can begin with officers relating how they come in contact with infants during their routine assignments. This will often result in stories of calls at which officers have discovered infants in various states of stress — for example, crying, wearing wet diapers, being hungry. Officers generally say that scenes such as these make them feel frustrated and disgusted. They identify with the infant, who is helpless and cannot care for herself or himself.

This leads into a discussion of what infants can and cannot do for themselves. Particular attention should be paid to the interplay among physical maturation, emotional development, and the protective role of the mother. All parenting — especially parenting of infants — requires that the adult acknowledge the difference between his or her need and that of the child and that the adult respond to the child's need. (No adult has a need to get up at 3

A.M. to change a diaper.) The instructors should encourage the class to address these issues.

It is more important that the class generate a list of what an infant needs than that the list be complete or comprehensive. This will lay the groundwork for the officers' active participation in the seminar. If instructors lecture while officers take notes, then the course will be less likely to achieve its goal of engaging officers in a new way of thinking.

Instructors may ask what kinds of responses officers usually receive when they address the needs of the infant along with those of the mother. This will often produce stories of neglectful and / or hostile mothers who mistook an officer's good intentions for criticism and who were dismissive and disrespectful of the officer without provocation. Officers can be helped to consider that the mother's response may not be about anything particular or personal about the officer. The mother may already be uncertain or uncomfortable about her treatment of the infant. These mixed feelings may lead her to react in a hostile manner in order to ward off her sense of her own inadequacy or "badness." She may also see the officer as someone who will remind her of that and make her feel bad as others have — perhaps her own parents.

Throughout this session, care should be taken to distinguish between abuse and neglect situations, in which infants are in life-threatening danger and must be reported to child welfare authorities, and situations in which officers are disgusted by the conditions under which they find children but there is no clear condition which would require that the case be reported.

There are no right answers in this discussion. Officers often recommend removal of the children from these disturbing home situations and bemoan the fact that child welfare authorities do not act according to officers' wishes. It is useful (and realistic) to leave this discussion to be continued at the next session.

*Case Vignette*

An officer is called to a domestic disturbance. A neighbor has reported loud arguing, threats, and a baby crying. After the officer repeatedly pounds on the door, a woman in her early twenties opens the door. She is wearing a housecoat, her hair is wild, her eyes are dull. The stereo is blasting. She is sullen and uncooperative. She denies any violence and says she is home alone with her two children, a two-year-old and a three-month-old. The apartment is dark and littered with takeout food boxes, dirty dishes, and dirty clothes. The children are sitting in front of the television on a filthy rug. The children's diapers are wet. The crying infant is holding an empty bottle, which the two-year-old takes to the mother. The mother tells the two-year-old to shut up and leave her alone.

## 3. SEPARATION AND TRAUMA:
### EIGHTEEN MONTHS TO THREE YEARS

### Key Concepts

- The role of a secure attachment to the psychological development of a child. John Bowlby (1988) writes about a "secure base" as necessary to the healthy development of children. The idea that this base is a person or persons — usually a child's parent or parents — is not obvious to some people. It needs to be developed through case examples, discussion, and/or videotape.
- What capacities are available to a very young child to cope with distress and/or trauma? The young child's increased physical abilities (walking, holding a cup and spoon), cognitive capacities (remembering and recognizing), language development (understanding what is said and

speaking), and the normal developmental struggles around feeling separate from the parents play a part — helpfully and negatively — in the child's response to separation or other trauma. Children who are overwhelmed by distress or trauma at this phase may exhibit eating and/or sleeping disturbances, attachment difficulties, and inconsolable crying.

- The other important mediator of the effects of trauma is the capacity of the parent to help the child cope. A parent's response to a child's distress has a significant impact on the child's responses because the parent represents the most significant base of security for the child of this age. When the parent is unavailable or absent, the child is further traumatized by the loss.

- Even very young children are capable of complex emotional reactions. Two-year-olds, for instance, can be depressed. They will demonstrate that in a manner consistent with their age and stage of development, through behavior, regression, crying, sleep or appetite disturbance, and so on.

## Process

This session examines the impact of separation on very young children (eighteen to thirty-six months), which is used as the model for the effect of trauma on children. These issues are addressed by exploring the question of what happens when a child's experience and feelings overwhelm her or his capacity to cope. It is useful in this session to extend this way of thinking to adults — that is, what is the impact of childhood trauma on adult capabilities and expectations, and what are the parallels to children who are overwhelmed and adults who feel in danger of being overwhelmed by their experiences?

The session builds directly on the previous session. There

may have been discussion of removal of an infant from the home in the previous session. What happens when young children are separated from their parents can then be a topic of this discussion.

One useful way to address this topic is by viewing the film *John* by James and Joyce Robertson (1969). This documentary about a seventeen-month-old English boy who is placed in a twenty-four-hour nursery for nine days while his mother has a second baby and recuperates details the daily changes in John as he becomes increasingly despondent and disorganized. It is the chronicle of his descent into a depression caused by separation.

The film provides an opportunity for officers to use their observational skills from a different perspective, that of the developmental observer. Officers can be asked to monitor John's actions and affects. They can see his attempts to engage adult caretakers and his gradual withdrawal due to the lack of response he receives. Adequate time should be allowed for discussion.

At the end of the session, the instructors might return to the discussion of removal and placement from the previous week's meeting about infants. A discussion of the balance between physical and emotional risk in the decisions officers and others make for children can be significant in setting the tone for the rest of the course.

### 4. YOUNG CHILDREN: FOUR TO SIX YEARS

#### Key Concepts

- The role of play as a means for children to express feelings and ideas about themselves and the world. For young children, symbolic and dramatic play is a way to enact and experiment with their ideas about themselves and the world. Increased cognitive capacity leads the young child to shift from the role of the toddler "explorer" who is discovering the world and learning about its properties to the role of "scientist" who is trying to figure out how things work, including one's family and oneself.

- The role of the child's growing awareness of his or her parents' relationship with each other and their separateness and independence from him or her. Along with the cognitive development of this stage comes the growing awareness that parents have relationships with each other and others which are not solely related to their roles as parents. This awareness is often expressed in sexual curiosity, anger, fantasies, and action aimed at feeling important and powerful like adults.

- What capacities are available to a young child to cope with distress and trauma? The toddler develops the use of language to express ideas and affects. Along with this improved ability to communicate, there is generally an increased capacity to cope with stress. The development of the use of language to convey thoughts and feelings rather than action is a key factor in the manner in which a child copes with impulses as he or she matures. A young child overwhelmed by stress or trauma may exhibit agitation, loss of previously attained developmental milestones around toilet training, repetitive nightmares, temper tantrums, and so on.

### Process

This session looks at the developing cognitive and symbolic capacities of young children (four- to six-year-olds) and how these capacities affect a child's ability to cope with internal and external stresses.

Because this session focuses on the child's inner world, it is useful for the clinician-instructor to present videotapes of young children in a play setting. These can be commercially available training tapes or tapes made in the instructor's institution. It may also be possible for the seminar group to observe young children in a nursery school or kindergarten classroom.

In addition to talking with officers about how they normally come in contact with children of this age, instructors can use tapes and/or in-person observations to move the conversation toward the child's inner life and fantasies. For example, watching a video-tape of a five-year-old only child play as if he had a baby sister can stimulate a discussion of the rivalry fantasies of children. Similarly, viewing a videotape of a child who is disturbed and anxious may foster a conversation about the importance of the developing ca-pacity of the young child to distinguish between fantasy and reality.

The observation skills of officers as they watch taped and/or live examples should lead to a discussion of the potential effects of various scenarios on young children—for example, the arrest of a parent, domestic violence, injury to a parent, to a child, to a friend, the problem of reliability of young children as witnesses in court. Such a discussion should include consideration of the kinds of interventions that could be helpful in situations like these. The first such intervention is the police officer's positive use of benign au-thority to provide safety and security. Other interventions, such as referral to a consultation service, can also be discussed.

### Case Vignette

During a routine patrol, an officer in a squad car observes a motorcyclist pass him at high speed. There is a small rider on the back of the bike. The officer does not chase the mo-torcyclist due to the potential danger to the rider and others, but later he sees the bike parked outside a convenience store. He pulls up and approaches the driver. He is angry that the driver of the motorcycle was a risk to himself, his rider, and

everyone else on the road at that time, including the officer.
He is going to write up the driver for every possible infrac-
tion. He notices that the rider is a five-year-old girl.

## 5. SCHOOL-AGE CHILDREN: SEVEN TO ELEVEN YEARS

### Key Concepts

- The continuum of psychological development. The pattern
  of development, with more complex responses to key
  issues — mastery and control, threat and defense, separation
  and individuation, self-awareness and self-esteem — can be
  reviewed during this session. It is important to emphasize
  the inclusive, or layered, model of development in which
  one stage builds on the next, rather than supplanting it.
- The role of sublimation, competition, and fairness. As the
  child's sexual interests and impulses develop, they often shift
  at this time to less direct expression, and the energy
  associated with these impulses is directed toward school,
  sports, and friends. The intensity of these impulses fuels the
  drive that underlies school achievement and athletic and
  peer competitiveness. Rules and a strong sense of what is
  fair and acceptable within the child's experience are
  connected to containing these impulses.
- The beginning of peer pressure. Peer group pressure begins
  relatively early, in some cases as early as third grade. The
  influence of older children and adolescents as role models
  is extremely powerful in these settings. The attitudes of
  children toward the police often begin to shift in a negative
  manner at this time.
- What capacities are available to a school-age child to cope
  with stress and trauma? As the school-age child continues to
  develop, she or he has increasing capacity to cope with stress

and trauma. These include the greater capacity to distinguish reality from fantasy and the increased ability to use language to moderate impulses and to express complicated ideas. These capacities are closely tied to the ability of parents and other significant adults to be supportive and protective. Some markers of being overwhelmed by stress or trauma are poorer academic performance, lying, stealing, fighting, sleep and eating disturbances, clinginess, and false bravado.

## Process

This session can begin by the instructor asking officers about their elementary school memories. They can be encouraged to recall what was important to them at that time and what they remember about their relationships with their families, their increasing sense of independence, their continuing sense of vulnerability, and where they looked for reassurance and security.

Officers can be asked about current experiences with children this age in their role as police. Particular attention should be paid to their thoughts about who and what they represent to children at this time.

Case scenarios should be developed which illustrate the key concepts for this session. At about this age children begin to be thought of as possibly helpful witnesses at crime scenes. Scenarios that explore the positive and problematic aspects of this, as well as some involving predelinquent activities, can be created and discussed.

### Case Vignettes
On a hot summer afternoon an eight-year-old boy "hangs out" with a sixteen-year-old neighbor whom he idolizes. The neighbor is playing basketball with another teenager

from the project where they live. An argument over a foul
begins to escalate into a fight. The other teenager takes a
gun out of his pocket. The sixteen-year-old yells for his
eight-year-old friend to run. They both run, and the sixteen-
year-old is shot in the back of the head and killed. The eight-
year-old runs home and tells his mother what happened.
She walks the boy back to the basketball court and tells an
officer whom she knows that her son was a witness. It is
later learned that this boy saw his father die of an accidental
shooting a year earlier.

In one neighborhood a group of nine-, ten-, and eleven-
year-old boys ambushes cars driving through the area with
super soaker water guns. When officers pull up to chase the
boys, they too are soaked as the boys escape laughing.

### 6. PUBERTY AND EARLY ADOLESCENCE

### Key Concepts

- The physical changes that are part of early adolescence — for
  example, the growth spurt, voice change, beginning of men-
  struation, breast development, and appearance of axillary,
  pubic, and facial hair — all have a powerful effect on the psychological development of the early adolescent. These
  changes make adolescents preoccupied with their bodies.
  There is often an attempt to control facial and bodily changes
  over which the adolescent feels no control, leading to an
  intense concern with hairdos, clothing, tattoos, and so on.
- The sexual issues that are part of early adolescence — for
  example, the increased focus on genital sexual gratification,
  increased propensity and capacity for masturbation, and the
  possibility of heterosexual and/or homosexual

experiences — all create potential discomfort, frustration, and anxiety.

- The reorganization of the self that is common in early adolescence. Along with the maturational and developmental issues, the adolescent must develop a sense of herself or himself as an individual who is distinct and independent. Relationships with parents and other authority figures often become the testing ground for this reorganization and establishment of a sense of self.

- Tensions between internal conflict and external behavior may be displaced and discharged in ways that can involve police officers, including fights, vandalism, harassment, and disturbances of the peace. Officers are better able to deal with these situations if they have an understanding of the developmental dynamics that contribute to the externalized problems.

- The effects of peer pressure. The peer group influence on the adolescent's view of the police and on the police's view of adolescents can be powerful and problematic. Officers need to consider both of these effects whenever they deal with adolescents.

- What capacities does a young adolescent have to cope with stress and trauma? As the young adolescent develops a better defined sense of himself or herself as a separate independent individual, his or her capacity to engage cognitive, physical, and experiential capacities in the service of coping with stress increases. A sense of the difference between reality and fantasy allows the adolescent to consider the difference between real and imagined fears stimulated by traumatic situations and to use positive identifications with strong and helpful adults to cope with those fears. Yet the wish to be adult and the physical resemblance to an adult may leave young adolescents particularly vulnerable to unrealistic feelings of guilt and inadequacy in the face of overwhelming situations. These feelings may lead to fearful, withdrawn behavior or to identifying with — or modeling behavior after — the aggressive delinquent activities of others.

## Process

As in the previous session, officers' life experiences can be helpful in the discussion. If a safe and comfortable atmosphere has been created, it should not be surprising if officers describe aspects of their own early adolescent struggles, which may also help older officers to recognize and understand the patterns of adolescent misconduct displayed by younger colleagues. This misconduct may have included drug experimentation and threatened violence, with lethal weapons rather than with fists and sticks, that was simply their generation's version of the adolescent acting out that the older officers engaged in when they were young. It is often helpful for instructors to discuss experiences from their own lives that illustrate the universality of developmental struggles. Even when initially embarrassing, trading stories, which are often ribald and funny, serves to help officers focus on the commonality of their experience with those of the adolescents with whom they come in contact on the job. Instructors can help officers move beyond simplistic distinctions about how it was different and better when they were growing up. One strategy is to ask officers to remember how they felt when their parents took that attitude with them.

As the universal issues of adolescent struggles emerge, instructors can move the conversation to scenarios out of the officers' experiences. By reviewing these, officers can be encouraged to come up with responses and interventions that are informed by knowledge of the developmental issues under consideration. For instance, when an officer is called to the scene of a knife fight between two pregnant teenage girls who are dueling over the father of their children, the officer cannot think only about separating the combatants, but can help each girl look for a friend or peer to vent her anger to safely and save face.

*Case Vignette*

A group of twelve-, thirteen-, and fourteen-year-olds sets fires in Dumpsters in the project where they live. They hide and laugh and call out as police and firefighters respond.

## 7. ISSUES OF RACE AND SOCIOECONOMIC STATUS IN CHILD DEVELOPMENT AND COMMUNITY POLICING

### Key Concepts

- Development occurs in a social context. The world in which children grow up affects their psychosocial development. Their sense of opportunity and hopefulness is in large part a reflection of the culture and society of contemporary America.
- Issues of class and race are both objective and subjective. Although there is little question that race and social class have profound effects on the experience of children and families, there are few, if any, universal certainties about these effects. Individuals experience and react differently to the same circumstances.
- Officers and clinicians bring their own experiences and reactions to the situations they confront as professionals. Individual backgrounds and responses are central to this session.

### Process

The purpose of this session is to bring to the forefront the idea that both child development and policing occur in a social context that has a powerful effect on the experiences of individuals and groups. The session is conceived of as a freewheeling discussion in which the instructors can pose provocative questions and act as facilitators of the discussion.

Some questions that have generated worthwhile conversation follow.

Is this a racist city? A classist city?

What does it feel like for an officer to deal with citizens and perpetrators of the same race? Of a different race?

Can a police officer be a role model for a child of a different race?

We have heard the phrase "poor people's medicine" to refer to the care that the uninsured receive. Is there such a thing as poor people's justice?

Can we really know the experiences of someone of another race or class? Is that important?

What process might help us learn about the experiences of people of another race, class, religion, region, or culture?


### 8. ADOLESCENCE

### Key Concepts

- Adolescence represents the revival and culmination of all of the developmental issues addressed thus far.
- A major feature of adolescence is that sexual and aggressive urges, along with the developmental movement toward autonomy and independence, can all be put into action in the world at large.
- What capacities does an adolescent have to cope with stress and trauma? As far as cognitive and physical maturation and development are concerned, an adolescent has the same equipment as an adult. However, adolescents' limited life experience and judgment make them vulnerable to stress and trauma as a threat to developmental progress. Adolescents who are overwhelmed by these situations may act like

younger children as they struggle to regain their psychological equilibrium. They may also seek self-centered or unhealthy short-sighted solutions to situations; these solutions can be physically dangerous to themselves and/or others.

### Process

This session lasts three hours and is devoted to viewing and discussing John Singleton's film *Boyz N the Hood* (Singleton, 1991). The film presents a view of adolescence in South Central Los Angeles which is rich in developmental detail.

The session can be introduced with a brief statement asking officers to watch the film with child and family developmental issues in mind. Afterward, the instructors lead a discussion in which officers are asked to compare their own adolescent experiences with those of the film's characters. Particular attention should be paid to the effects of family experiences, issues of developing independence, sexuality, peer group influence, and perceptions of hope and opportunity.

The aim of the session is to promote thoughtful discussion of the relationships between police officers and adolescents from multiple viewpoints. It is inevitable that there will be a wide range of opinions and feelings within the group. The success of this session should be measured in the appreciation of complexity and uncertainty that the discussion reflects.

### 9. CONCLUSION: COMMUNITY MENTAL HEALTH RESOURCES AND COURSE EVALUATION

#### Key Concepts

- Officers need to know about the local mental health resources for children so that they can make appropriate referrals.

- Evaluation and review of the seminars will help plan future training for others in the police department and for further training of officers who have completed this series.

## Process

This session begins with the distribution of a handout listing all community mental health resources with telephone numbers, names of contact staff, and brief program and eligibility descriptions. Officers should be encouraged to share any previous experiences with these agencies with the group.

Following the discussion of resources, instructors can lead a review of the course and ask officers for their assessments of the strengths and weaknesses of the course. This can be framed as what they would like to spend more time on and what aspects could be shortened or eliminated.

If there is to be formal post-training evaluation, it can occur at the end of this session.

MIRIAM BERKMAN
STEVEN MARANS
DOUGLAS MACDONALD

# 4 Consultation Service

Police officers, who are the first on the scene and most regularly in contact with children and families exposed to community violence, are in a unique position to intervene to ameliorate the psychological consequences of children's chronic experience of violence. Officers' stabilizing presence offers distressed children and their parents a sense of security and safety. The consultation service of the CD-CP program is intended to provide case-by-case assistance to officers in support of this role.

## BASIC ELEMENTS OF THE CONSULTATION SERVICE

The consultation service provides a wide range of coordinated clinical and police responses, including round-the-clock availability, crisis response, coordination of community response, clinical referral, interagency collaboration, home-based follow-up, and officer support.

### On-Call Availability

A team of clinicians and supervisory officers is available on twenty-four-hour call to consult with officers in the field. The clinicians who staff the consultation service are the designated collaborators from the mental health agency, a group known to officers from the training seminars and from their regular presence at scenes of police activity. The police who staff the service are officers who have completed the fellowship program and have developed both special expertise in dealing with children and families and close working relationships with the collaborating clinicians. At least one clinician and one officer are available to respond in person at all times. It is important that officers in need of consultation may call either a fellow officer or a clinician, as they find most appropriate or comfortable, and that the police and mental health members of the consultation service team involve each other in their responses as needed. If possible, on-call staff can be provided with a mobile telephone for both safety and accessibility.

### Direct Clinical Response

Calls from officers to the consultation service may lead to immediate clinical interviews with victims or witnesses of violence, or to telephone consultations between clinicians, officers, and parents, with arrangements made to see a child the following day.

Depending on the urgency of the situation and the safety and convenience of the child and family, clinicians may see children at the scene of the incident, the police station, the mental health clinic, the hospital, or the child's home, school, or another community site.

*Case Vignettes*

An eight-year-old boy witnessed his mother's shooting as she answered the door late at night. The child's grandmother took care of the boy while his mother was admitted to the hospital. The consultation service clinician was informed by the referring officer that the child was safe and asleep. The clinician arranged with the child's grandmother to see the child the next day.

Several children witnessed a man's being stabbed by a female acquaintance during an evening card game. Both assailant and victim fled from the scene. When the police arrived, a nine-year-old boy was silently hiding behind a bookcase and several younger children were clinging to their mother or talking repetitively about what they had seen. A sergeant from the consultation service called a clinician. Two clinicians came immediately to the family's home, met with the children and their mother, and arranged follow-up sessions for two of the children the next day.

## Coordination of Community Response

When emergency calls to the consultation service involve incidents witnessed by large numbers of children, police and clinical staff may take the lead in coordinating the responses of other community institutions like schools, churches, fire department, and community advocates, so as to minimize the traumatic effect of the event on the children and their families. When calls concern many children and families, consultation service clinicians may see children and parents in groups rather than individually and should involve other clinical staff of the collaborating mental health agency in their response as needed.

*Case Vignette*

A fifteen-year-old boy at the periphery of a drug-dealing operation was shot and killed in a crowded housing project. No witnesses to the event were identified immediately. In the following days, crowds of distraught teenagers gathered on the street at the scene of the killing, and local merchants and neighbors complained that they were causing a disturbance. The district police supervisor, a CD-CP fellow, directed officers under his command not to arrest the youths and instead invited them to the local substation for a series of discussions focused on the grief associated with their friend's death and the general frustration and hopelessness regarding opportunities for young people in the community. Subsequent to these meetings, the supervisor contacted parents he knew and worked with them to organize a meeting for the teenagers with representatives of job training services. During this process the supervisor had also been consulting with a CD-CP clinician, who made her services available to parents to discuss their children's reactions to the shooting. (For additional examples, see chapters 5 and 7.)

## Clinical Referral

Referrals are made to other appropriate clinical services like emergency rooms, inpatient facilities, and outpatient clinics. Telephone consultation may assist officers in determining when children should be brought to the emergency room, when the local child welfare agency should be contacted, or when a child should be referred to a clinician who is already involved with the child or family. In cases not so urgent as to require his or her immediate, on-scene presence, the consultation service clinician should be able to facilitate a prompt referral to an outpatient clinician from the collaborating mental health agency. In other cases in which the consultation service staff respond directly, their clinical assessments may lead to a range of referrals to other clinical services both within and outside the collaborating mental health organization. (See guidelines below regarding child welfare referrals.)

### Case Vignettes

A nine-year-old boy witnessed the fatal shooting of an eighteen-year-old family friend. In the course of consultation service contact, the boy revealed that he had been at the scene of several other violent crimes, including the stabbing death of his father. In spite of a history of poor school performance and multiple problems at home, the referral by police officers was the first opportunity for mental health assessment, which led to longer term outpatient treatment.

A ten-year-old boy witnessed the shooting of a relative in his apartment. The child and his mother were seen by a consultation service clinician for four sessions at home to assess their response to the incident and to provide support during the crisis. When both child and mother continued to experience serious symptoms of sleep disturbance, hyperarousal, intrusive thoughts of the incident, and restricted daily activities, both were referred to the collaborating mental health agency for outpatient psychotherapy.

A fourteen-year-old boy stabbed an adult man in the course of a violent domestic dispute between the man and his girlfriend. The man fled the scene. Several days later, an officer, who knew the boy from previous encounters involving reports of domestic violence in the boy's family, called the consultation service to discuss her concerns about the boy. When the clinician learned that the boy had been hospitalized recently following a suicide attempt, the clinician determined that it would be important for the boy's current therapist to be informed of the event and available to the boy, rather than to introduce a new therapist to the child and family at a time of acute stress. The clinician therefore recommended that the officer obtain permission to contact the boy's therapist. The CD-CP clinician remained in a consultative role with both the officer and the treating clinician.

## Interagency Collaboration

Consultation service staff collaborate with other service providers already involved with the child or family, such as school personnel, therapists, pediatricians, and child welfare professionals. Many children referred to the consultation service will already have established relationships with other clinical service providers who also have a wealth of knowledge about the child's family, history, environment, and previous functioning. Consultation service staff can use information provided by these other professionals to understand the child's presentation following exposure to an acute episode of violence in the context of the child's previous experiences and can assist the professionals who will be involved with a child and family in the long term to respond to the child's distress over time. In cases involving the child welfare system, the consultation service may provide clinical assessments that inform placement decisions or may collaborate with child welfare professionals in arranging treatment and other referrals.

### Case Vignettes
A six-year-old girl woke up to find her mother dead of a drug overdose. Police at the scene called the consultation

service clinician and the local child welfare agency. The clinician consulted with child welfare personnel about the best emergency placement for the child, provided a clinical assessment to inform the agency's long-term planning for the child, and assisted the child's aunt in understanding the child's behavior and supporting the child following her mother's death. After the child was permanently with her aunt, the clinician arranged a referral for treatment to a mental health agency near their home.

During a crippling snowstorm, an eleven-year-old boy witnessed the fatal shooting of a neighbor in the child's apartment. An officer-clinician team from the consultation service met immediately with the child and his mother to discuss the incident and the child's reactions. When the consultation service team learned that the child was home for the weekend from a residential treatment center, the team provided coverage for the mother and child while snowbound over the weekend, then provided the boy's regular therapist with information about the boy's clinical status upon his return and consulted with treatment center staff about how best to support him upon his return home.

A thirteen-year-old boy was arrested repeatedly for a series of property offenses and assaults on younger children. Officers referred the boy to the consultation service and an outpatient evaluation was arranged. Based on the boy's lack of impulse control and the absence of effective parental supervision, the evaluator recommended residential treatment and referred the family to the local child welfare agency. When child welfare workers refused to place the boy in a residential setting, the clinician obtained the family's permission to collaborate with the district police supervisor, a

CD-CP fellow, in advocating with both juvenile justice and child welfare authorities for an appropriate placement.

## Home-Based Follow-Up

Follow-up contacts with the child and family can be made by the consultation service clinician or fellow, the officer who responded to the complaint, or any of them when it is thought that this would be helpful and acceptable to the family. Clinicians may provide brief treatment to assist the child in resolving post-traumatic symptoms as well as extended assessments to determine if longer term psychotherapy or more intensive clinical intervention is called for. Officers may support a child's recovery through regular visits that reassure the child and family of the officer's continued presence in the neighborhood and concern for the child's well-being. The officer may also provide concrete information regarding the progress of an investigation or measures that could increase the family's safety. In addition, follow-up visits by officers provide opportunities to reintroduce the availability of clinical services to parents who declined an offer of service at the time of the incident but later find their children to be experiencing difficulties.

### Case Vignettes

A six-year-old girl witnessed her mother's being robbed at gunpoint in their backyard. A consultation service clinician saw the child and family that day at home and for three follow-up sessions in the clinic. The community-based sergeant, who was a CD-CP fellow, also made a follow-up visit to the family at home, discussed with them police information about a series of robberies in the neighborhood, and suggested ways to increase the security of the yard.

An eleven-year-old and a two-year-old witnessed the shooting death of a relative in their apartment. Immediately following the incident, the children's mother declined a clinical referral but accepted a community-based sergeant's business card with his beeper number. In the week following the shooting, the sergeant made several follow-up visits to the family to express concern for the children and to inform the family of the shooter's arrest. When the mother was overwhelmed by fears that the shooter would return, she called the sergeant on the beeper. Ten days after the shooting, the mother accepted the sergeant's renewed suggestion of a clinical referral.

### Officer Support

Consultation service staff, including both supervisory officers and clinicians, routinely follow up with the officers who call for consultation or assistance in order to provide information about the outcome of the officer's referral, to consult about any further action that the officer might take to assist the referred family, and to respond to any concerns that the officer might have regarding the incident. In especially difficult cases, like those involving death or injury to a child, consultation service staff should pay particular attention to the emotional responses of the officers involved. Ongoing support is essential to enable officers to function optimally, including continuing to take notice of children's emotional distress.

#### Case Vignettes
A seven-year-old boy was hit and killed by a car while three friends watched. Three officers and a clinician from the consultation service met that afternoon at the scene of the accident with the uninjured boys. After this meeting, the officers and the clinician returned to the local substation to discuss both the children's and their own reactions to the events and to plan follow-up sessions with the children and their parents.

A seven-month-old baby was killed by a stray bullet that came through an apartment window. The scene was gruesome, and officers at the scene were visibly shaken. A clinician from the consultation service went to the scene to offer support to the supervisor on duty and to consult with him about assisting other officers in coping with the incident. In turn, the supervisor went to unusual lengths to arrange time for his officers to discuss the experience and, where necessary, facilitated referrals for additional support. The incident also stimulated an ongoing discussion in the CD-CP program conference about how best to deliver essential emotional support to officers who witness traumatic scenes of violence.

## GUIDELINES FOR OPERATING A CONSULTATION SERVICE

As part of the process of developing a CD-CP consultation service, the collaborating police department and mental health agency will have to develop specific operating procedures. It is important that the police and clinical staff who will be most involved in the day-to-day operation of the service participate in developing the procedures. The following are some of the specific issues that program developers may confront in establishing a consultation service and some guidelines for their resolution.

### Criteria for Referral

Each program must establish criteria for referral to the consultation service. The basic referral criteria should be as follows: the presence of a child on the scene of a visibly violent incident, whether the child was a participant in the violence, a victim, or a witness; or the death of an immediate member of a child's household due to unnatural causes, including homicide, suicide, and accident, whether or not the child was present.

It is recommended that criteria for required referrals be read broadly — to include anytime a child is in an apartment where a domestic incident occurs — rather than restrictively — only incidents seen directly by children or only those resulting in injuries of a given degree. Despite the increased demands that broad referral criteria make on the time and emotional investment of the consulting clinicians and supervisory officers, inclusive referral criteria are preferred because they facilitate learning and collaboration between police and mental health professionals, and also because they offer greater opportunity for clinical consultation in cases where children are not obviously distressed but may be far more affected by their exposure to violence than the adults around them wish to believe.

Use of the service may be expanded further if officers are encouraged to seek consultation in other circumstances in which they believe a child is in distress. For example, officers might seek consultation in such situations as:

- a child is known to an officer to be considering joining or withdrawing from a gang;
- a child confides in an officer about his or her emotional distress, which is unrelated to violence or other criminal activity;
- a child is observed by an officer to be habitually truant; or
- a child is known by an officer to live in a household in which the adults abuse drugs or engage in other disturbing behavior.

These situations may not require the same emergency response as cases involving acute exposure to violence; however, officers may find support and guidance from the consultation service valuable in making clinical referrals or in planning their own responses to the child and family.

## Process of Referral

Several different modes of referral may be appropriate, depending on the urgency of the incident.

*Emergency referrals are made by telephone, beeper, or radio* to a clinician on call or to a police officer on the consultation service. Emergency referrals may come from any officer in the department, including the first officer on the scene, the supervisor on the scene, and the detective assigned to the investigation. Supervisors may want to take responsibility for calling the consultation service in order to streamline officers' dealing with the service. There is no paperwork required to initiate an emergency referral. In New Haven, all police officers carry a business card listing the names and telephone and beeper numbers of all CD-CP clinicians. The back of the card reads:

> REMINDER
> Anytime you encounter a child who has either
> *lost a household family member to unnatural death OR been on the scene of a visibly violent crime*
> you must beep either an officer or a clinician from the Child Development–Community Policing Consultation Service. In situations involving the possibility of child abuse or neglect, you still have a legal obligation to call DCF [state Department of Children and Families].

If there is any question whether to make a referral or whether to use the emergency referral process, officers should be encouraged to call and to use the beeper service. Nonemergency calls can be prioritized by the consultation service staff and addressed later.

After receiving a referral, the clinician or officer discusses the situation with other members of the consultation service, if appropriate, formulates a plan of action, and requests the assistance of other clinicians and/or officers, as needed.

*Nonemergency referrals can be made by telephone* to a clinical coordinator from the participating mental health agency who is designated by the core group of clinicians to receive and respond to nonemergency requests for service. The clinical coordinator should respond as soon as possible to an officer's request for consultation and should arrange a clinical contact with the child and family.

*Nonemergency referrals can be made in writing on referral forms that are available to officers in police stations.* Written referrals may be particularly useful for less urgent referrals that take place at night, when officers may be reticent to use the beeper service. Officers who are involved in the CD-CP program are responsible for collecting and transmitting completed referral forms to the clinical coordinator or to the program conference. Once received, written referrals are treated the same as nonemergency telephone referrals. (See figure 4.1 for a copy of the referral form used in New Haven.)

### Engaging Families with the Consultation Service

Officers who staff the consultation service provide valuable support to children and families by introducing the availability of clinical services following a traumatic incident. Officers should be prepared to suggest to parents that children will benefit from an opportunity to meet with an experienced clinician to "talk or play." It is important for officers to recognize that initially many parents will not be aware of the psychological effects that exposure to scenes of violence may have on their children, particularly since this awareness confronts parents with the difficulty of protecting their children, the pain of the parent's own helplessness in the face of danger, and, in some cases, guilt regarding the parent's own participation in the frightening events.

In introducing the consultation service, officers can assist adults to recognize:

- that exposure to violence is upsetting both for children and for parents;
- that children may have feelings that they express through their behavior rather than in words, or that they do not express right away;
- that there is a service available to help the parent and the child cope with the feelings raised by their experiences; and
- that the service is voluntary and intended to assist them in responding to their children, unlike a referral to child protective services, which will often be experienced as punitive.

Clinicians who respond to emergency referrals should be prepared to take active steps to engage families with mental health services. Home visits and multiple follow-up telephone calls may be necessary in cases in which parents are immobilized following exposure to danger, as well as in cases in which families are alienated or suspicious of professional helpers.

Clinicians may reiterate the introductory information provided by police officers, clarifying that exposure to violence is upsetting for children and adults, that children often have very different responses to their experiences than adults, and that experience has shown that talking about their feelings can help both children and adults cope with upsetting events.

Clinicians should aim to provide a forum in which traumatized children and adults can begin to master their overwhelming sense of helplessness by putting their experiences into words and by differentiating the reality of the events from fantasies of responsibility, blame, and revenge. By providing parents with basic information about children's expectable responses to traumatic

Figure 4.1. Referral Form for Yale Child Study Center

DATE OF REFERRAL _____ DATE OF INCIDENT _____

TIME OF INCIDENT _____

LOCATION OF INCIDENT _____

TYPE OF INCIDENT _____

CHILD OR CHILDREN TO BE REFERRED

| NAME | D.O.B. | ADDRESS | TEL. # | SEX |
|------|--------|---------|--------|-----|
|      |        |         |        |     |
|      |        |         |        |     |
|      |        |         |        |     |
|      |        |         |        |     |
|      |        |         |        |     |

PARENT OR GUARDIAN OF CHILD OR CHILDREN
TO BE REFERRED

| NAME | ADDRESS | TEL. # |
|------|---------|--------|
|      |         |        |
|      |         |        |
|      |         |        |

```
COMMENTS AND/OR AREAS OF CONCERN: _____

_____

_____

_____

_____

_____

OFFICER'S NAME _____

BADGE # _____ DISTRICT _____
```

events, clinicians also can support parents in their efforts to assist their children.

Clinicians should listen carefully to the child and/or parent describe the experience in an effort to understand the individual meaning that each child attributes to events, in light of the child's developmental phase and previous life experience. It is important that clinicians not assume that traumatic experiences are determined by the specific details of the violence witnessed or that there are standardized clinical responses that will be helpful to all children and families. (See chapter 7 regarding program results and associated bibliography for detailed descriptions of clinical intervention strategies for children exposed to traumatic violence. The appendix contains a questionnaire that may be used to guide interviews with parents regarding children's post-traumatic symptoms.)

### Follow-Up with Officers

Clinicians who become involved with children and families in response to officers' referrals should contact the referring officer for three main reasons:

- to let the officer know there has been a clinical response;
- to discuss any ongoing contact by the officer that might be helpful to the child or family, for example, follow-up visits; and
- to learn the status of the investigation or background information about the family or neighborhood that may assist the clinician in understanding the child's presentation.

Follow-up conversations between officers and mental health professionals provide opportunities for relationships to develop in the context of collaborative work on individual cases. Difficult cases present valuable opportunities for police and clinicians to learn more about the possibilities and limitations of their own and the other's profession and provide opportunities for professionals of both disciplines to recognize and discuss their individual reactions to the frustrating and painful situations that confront them in their work.

### Clinical Staffing

A well-functioning consultation service requires sufficient clinical staff to be available to respond to emergency calls on a twenty-four-hour basis, to conduct clinic- and community-based assessments and short-term interventions, and to have access to longer term clinical services for referral of children who experience more serious difficulties. Staffing is complicated by the inevitable inconsistency of the volume of calls, as well as wide variation in the intensity and duration of the appropriate clinical response. Some considerations include the following.

*On-call staff.* The clinicians who are the designated central collaborators from the mental health agency should establish a rotation for responding to emergency calls. Limiting the responsibility for emergency response to this core group facilitates the development of relationships between officers and these clinicians and affords opportunities for a small group of clinicians to develop greater knowledge regarding the range of police responses to violent incidents and the immediate clinical presentation of children and families exposed to violence and trauma. On-call responsibility should be shared among the central group of clinicians. It is recommended that each clinician carry the beeper for periods of one or two weeks so that follow-up calls regarding an incident can be more readily answered by the same clinician.

*Short-term intervention.* Initial clinical contacts, assessments, and brief clinical interventions can be made by the central collaborators or by other experienced clinicians from the participating mental health agency. It is important that an expanded group of clinicians be available to respond to emergency and nonemergency referrals so that all referrals can be covered promptly. Response to referrals from the consultation service should be counted as *part of*, not as *additional to* a staff member's expected clinical load at the mental health agency. Clinical staff should be available to respond independently or in pairs or groups, depending on the number of children and parents involved in a particular incident.

*Case load.* Some programs may assign clinicians to staff the consultation service in addition to other clinical responsibilities at the collaborating mental health agency and some may assign clinicians to the CD-CP program full-time. In both cases, case-load limits should be established with consideration given to the clinical complexity and emotional intensity of many of the cases referred through the consultation service.

*Consultation and supervision.* It is important that mental health professionals who respond to referrals from the consultation service have ample opportunities for consultation and supervision with other clinicians as well as opportunities for discussion with officers who are involved in the cases. Frequent consultation between clinicians and officers provides essential support for both kinds of professionals coping with the intense and disturbing feelings that are aroused by close involvement with traumatized children and families. Some of these issues may be addressed in the regular CD-CP program conference, some in collaboration meetings with officers, and some in individual clinical supervision.

### Confidentiality

Collaborative work by police and mental health professionals raises issues of confidentiality and professional boundaries in individual cases. Some considerations include the following situations of sharing information. Collaborators are advised to consult with legal counsel in order to clarify the particular legal requirements of their own jurisdiction.

Follow-up conversations between officers and clinicians are intended to further the goals of developing and implementing collaborative interventions and supporting officers in their interactions with children and families. As in the case of other referral sources, officers should be provided with prompt and respectful acknowledgment that their referrals have been received and that contact has been established with the child and family. Clinical interviews are confidential. Clinicians may discuss with officers general information that the officer can use to enhance the officer's further contact with individual children and families, for example, a child's generalized fearfulness and the usefulness of an officer's visits in reestablishing a sense of security. Specific clinical information can also be shared with appropriate permission. Despite the generally collaborative nature of the CD-CP program's work, some children and families will require a purely clinical intervention, which relies on strict boundaries of confidentiality for the establishment of a trusting therapeutic relationship. Clinicians should be prepared to engage in open discussions with officers regarding the parameters of their interdisciplinary exchange of information and the reasons for maintaining clinical confidentiality.

Clinical referrals in cases where there are ongoing criminal investigations have a special potential for conflict of interest and present risks both to the necessary confidentiality of criminal investigations and to the maintenance of therapeutic relationships. If a child or parent who is referred for clinical intervention is also the subject of a criminal investigation, officers and clinicians involved in the case ordinarily should not speak to each other about the case without the express written permission of the parent (and the child if he or she is an older adolescent).

In cases involving ongoing criminal investigations (for example, concerning a juvenile who is accused of serious or repetitive violent activity or a parent who is accused of harming a child), it is also advisable for consultation service clinicians to consider carefully whether it is more appropriate to offer confidential voluntary services, or to act in a nontherapeutic consultative role in which information may be shared with the police and/or other agencies for the purpose of joint decision making about the child's needs. Clinicians and officers should be aware that in some circumstances a child's or parent's immediate need for clinical intervention will conflict with the interests of the criminal justice system in using clinical data to inform court-ordered dispositions; in these cases, difficult decisions must be made regarding which role the consultation service staff will assume. Once a confidential clinical relationship has been offered, the content of clinical interviews may not be disclosed without permission, except as required by state laws regarding the reporting of child abuse or to prevent serious injury to the patient or another person.

Some referrals to the consultation service may lead to a clinician's primary role being that of a consultant to the police, to a court, or to the local child welfare agency, rather than being in a therapeutic role. In these circumstances, the clinician involved in the case should explicitly tell the child and family that the purpose of contact is as a consultant to an agency and that any discussions with the clinician are therefore not confidential.

It is also important for police and mental health professionals to be explicit with each other regarding the consulting clinician's role in a particular case. In some situations (a complex investigation of injuries to a young child, for instance), officers may request consultation and advice for themselves about how to understand a child's statements or behavior or how to understand other clinical reports as an aid to investigation, rather than request direct clinical intervention for the child. In other situations, officers may request assistance in pursuing a prompt and clinically appropriate disposition for a juvenile delinquent and may therefore request a forensic evaluation. Clinicians may also suggest that they assume nontherapeutic consultative roles in some cases. A variety of roles may be appropriate at different times. However, a clinician usually cannot assume multiple roles in the same case without violating a patient's trust or becoming embroiled in a conflict of interest (Goldstein et al., 1986). Police officers may often not be familiar with the limits of various clinical roles or the implications of the clinician's assumption of one role or another. Therefore, clinicians should be prepared to engage officers in considering what role is most appropriate and to articulate and maintain the boundaries of whatever role is chosen.

### Child Welfare Referrals

Some cases referred to the consultation service concern children who have been or who are at risk of being abused, neglected, or abandoned by adult caregivers. These cases raise questions about referral to child welfare authorities. The criteria for mandated child welfare referrals by police and mental health professionals are governed by state law. State authorities are responsible for making decisions regarding the removal and placement of children. Referrals by police officers to the CD-CP consultation service do not substitute for mandated referrals to the appropriate child welfare agency. In situations where it is difficult to determine whether child welfare reports are warranted, consultation service staff may assist officers. If requested, consultation service staff may also collaborate with child welfare professionals by providing clinical assessments and / or arranging appropriate therapeutic services for children and parents.

JEAN ADNOPOZ
RICHARD RANDALL
STEVEN MARANS

# 5  Program Conference

The multiple activities of the Child Development–Community Policing Program suggest a need for a structured and consistent means of integrating the diverse program elements into a coherent whole. Keeping track of all the components — departmentwide training in the basic principles of child development, the fellowship program, clinical consultation around problematic cases, and crisis intervention, assessment, and treatment for children affected by violence and traumatic stress — requires ongoing discussion and coordination. Experience has made clear that the potential stresses and pressures inherent in this kind of work demand built-in opportunities for police officers and clinicians not only to discuss the actions and concerns of the previous week, but also to place these actions and concerns in the broader context of the program.

The success of the CD-CP program requires a forum for the sharing of information across these related but distinct domains in order to coordinate planning on both the individual case and program level; address the management, housekeeping, and administrative functions of the program; and support the collaboration by continuously assessing the program's strengths and weaknesses in the interest of enhancing its effectiveness.

The structure that best addresses these concerns is the program conference, a weekly meeting that provides a forum through which the continuity and coherence of the CD-CP program can be maintained over time. It is here that the program's goals of applying the principles of human development and functioning to policing strategies, concepts, and activities can best be brought together and the roles and tasks of all the players identified and understood. The program conference offers a consistent and reliable opportunity for the police officers and mental health clinicians who staff the program to meet together to:

- review cases in order to understand better the experiences of children and families affected by violence;
- integrate and apply police and mental health principles and strategies in order to develop improved methods of collaboration and response;
- identify and address systemic, institutional, and policy issues that may affect the ability of the CD-CP program to meet its goals;
- address administrative matters as they arise; and
- build the personal, trusting relationships between the police fellows and the clinicians which are essential to the program's success.

The conference provides a forum in which both police fellows and clinicians can gain a better understanding of the application of the program's principles to the institutions and systems they represent. Clinicians have the opportunity to learn firsthand and in greater detail about the social context and circumstances of the lives of children affected by violence and stress — children whom many have previously encountered only in the examining room. Police officers are given the opportunity to integrate their knowledge of what happens on the street and in the neighborhoods with what they have learned about the developmental process and the dynamic interplay between children's external reality and their innermost wishes and strivings. In the program conference the pieces of the CD-CP program come together.

A single meeting of the program conference may focus upon any or all of the areas outlined above. It is recommended that during every meeting time is set aside for the presentation and discussion of cases referred for consultation during the preceding week as well as for a review of other ongoing cases that continue to be served by the project in addition to any other relevant matters. The program conference should be a required meeting, attended by the police fellows and the clinicians assigned to the CD-CP program. The recommended length of the meeting is ninety minutes.

The components of the program conference are as follows.

## CASE REVIEW

Each weekly program conference should include a case review segment in which cases of specific children who were affected by violence, either as victims or as witnesses, are presented. The primary purpose of the case review is to develop a case plan that builds upon the particular knowledge and expertise of the police and the clinicians, coordinates the plan of intervention, and leads to a shared understanding of the needs of the individual child or adolescent and family whose case is under discussion. During the time devoted to case review, cases previously presented to the group should be updated as often as is appropriate.

The case review segment of the conference is led by a senior clinician who — through careful examination of the material — brings into view the pertinent clinical and systems issues inherent in each case. The case material should be presented jointly by both the clinician who responded to the case — whether for consultation or direct contact with the child — and the officer who has the greatest familiarity with the initial report to the police and the subsequent activity. Clinical case presentations are most effective when presenters follow a standard outline which captures: significant demographic data; social, medical, and educational information; and current and previous police contact concerning the child or adolescent. The police officer begins the presentation with a description of the initial report in which the nature of the call for service and the available information about the affected children is described, including their histories and the history of the family (if known to the police), the immediate effect of the incident on the children and family, and the immediate police response.

### Questions To Be Answered by the Police

1. Describe the nature of the incident as it was reported to your department. What happened? Who was affected?
2. Describe what you know about the child(ren) affected by the incident. What do you know about their ages, gender, family history, past involvement with the police?
3. Describe what was done by the police in response. Who was involved? Was a referral made to the Child Development–Community Policing Program? If not, why not?
4. What are the recommendations for case planning at this time?

If the child or adolescent and family has already been seen by a clinician, the clinician continues the presentation with a further description of the child's functioning following the initial incident, with particular attention to the behavioral and psychological reactions to the trauma.

### Questions To Be Answered by the Clinician

1. What was the nature of the clinician contact — consultation only or direct clinical contact? How soon following the incident did the contact take place?
2. If there was direct contact with the child, describe the child's presentation.
3. Describe what is known about the child's earlier functioning within and across multiple settings, including school, home, and community, and with peers.
4. Describe what is known about the child's medical, behavioral, and psychological functioning.
5. Describe what appears to be the nature of the family's relationships at present.
6. Describe what appears to have been the impact of the reported incident on the functioning of the family unit.
7. What strengths can be identified and what needs to be supported in the family environment? What areas of functioning appear to be the most problematic?
8. What are the recommendations for case planning at this time?

Following the presentation of case material, the senior clinician engages the members of the group in a discussion with the aim of developing a case plan that integrates the work of the officer and the clinician, delineates the roles to be played by the two agencies in the process of intervention and follow-up, and enriches the understanding of the individual case and illuminates the issues inherent in the case which have application to other areas of the program. Cases are then reviewed on an ongoing basis in order to assess the effects of services and to reformulate intervention strategies, as needed.

Some possible topics that can be used to organize this discussion follow.

- Can the system of care devise flexible, appropriate, and easily accessible ways of responding to the child's and family's needs?
- Who will be expected to develop an alliance with the child and family? Is there an existing relationship between the family and the community-based police officer which can be utilized in serving this family?
- How will services be coordinated? How will roles and tasks be assigned?
- Are there other resources that should be involved? Are they available?
- Who will take primary responsibility for this case, monitor its progress, and bring it back to the program conference for follow-up?
- What has been learned from this case?

The following cases were adapted from incidents reported at a weekly program conference.

*Case 1* A police officer reported that at 8 P.M. one evening, a woman, approximately twenty-five years of age, ran to a police substation to report that two adults were stabbing each other in an apartment directly across from the station. When the officer entered the home, he found a blood-stained dining-room floor, a discarded deck of cards on the dining-room table, and eight children scattered throughout the apartment, including a nine-year-old boy huddled in a corner. The man and woman involved in the stabbing had left the scene.

The officer learned that the children ranged in age from three months to nine years. Four children lived in the apartment, and four were visiting. Both sets of parents were present. The stabbings had occurred in full view of the children. The officer spoke to the parents of his concern about the children's reaction to the violence they had witnessed and offered to contact a clinician. The visiting parents did not accept an immediate referral but agreed to take information about the CD-CP program. The parents who lived in the apartment accepted the officer's suggestion that a clinician visit the home that evening. The officer contacted the clinician by beeper.

The clinician reported that she and a colleague arrived at the home soon after receiving the call from the officer. Upon their arrival, the officer explained what had happened and provided information from his observation of the children. The nine-year-old, who was still huddled in a corner, appeared most dramatically affected. One clinician worked directly with this boy, while the other clinician and a supervisory officer, a CD-CP fellow, spoke to both parents and children about their reactions to what had occurred. With the clinician's support, the nine-year-old was able to tell what he had experienced, placing particular emphasis on his worries about his mother's safety and possible separation from her.

After discussion, the family agreed that the clinician would continue to visit them and assess the need for further intervention. The officer would also stop by to see how things were going. The case was scheduled to be reviewed at the next program conference.

*Case 2*  An officer reported that a fire broke out in a public
housing project early on a Saturday morning. Residents
heard a woman screaming that her babies were trapped,
someone called 911, and police and fire personnel were dis-
patched to the scene. When the police arrived, the badly
burned woman had jumped from a window. Firefighters entered the building and located the children. The younger
boy, aged six months, was dead at the scene, and the two-
year-old was taken by ambulance to the hospital, where he
could not be revived. All of the events, including the removal
of the children's burned bodies from the apartment, took
place in full view of a large group of children and adults. Police at the scene called a supervisor who had completed the
CD-CP fellowship, and the supervisor called two clinicians.

The clinician reported that he and a colleague arrived
about an hour after the fire had been brought under control.
Police and fire personnel were investigating the scene.
Adults and children were sitting on the steps of the buildings
in small groups describing the horrible sights they had seen,
lamenting the deaths, and complaining about the poor condition of the apartments and the slow response of emergency
personnel. The clinicians introduced themselves to some of
the residents who were eager to include them in the discussion. Police officers arranged for a community room to be
opened so that the clinicians would have a place to meet
with residents who wished to talk about their own and their
children's experiences. One clinician met with a group of
about fifteen children ranging in age from four to eleven,
while the other clinician met with a smaller group of parents.

Many children were eager to tell what they had seen
and described frightening scenes of burning bodies and
helpless onlookers. With the clinician's help, children described feeling frightened and sad, worried that something

would happen to them or to their parents, and angry that adults (who were supposed to keep children safe) had not protected the children who died. In their group, the parents focused primarily on their worries that their own apartments might not be safe and on whom to blame for the tragedy. The clinician discussed with the parents some of their children's likely responses and ways the parents could support their children's recovery.

At the program conference, plans were made to address both the ongoing clinical needs of the children who had witnessed the fire and the residents' experience of being powerless and ignored by municipal services, including the police. The discussion centered on ways the police might use the disaster as an opportunity to forge better relations with the community, emphasizing the police role in delivering clinical services and supporting the creation of other neighborhood-based, child-focused activities. The police department subsequently organized a series of meetings of fire, housing, mental health, and city officials, as well as meetings between officials and concerned residents. In addition to delivering clinical services to the community, the police mobilization of other agencies led to a review of housing and fire safety standards, as well as immediate inspection of all units in the housing complex, in response to community concerns.

## Confidentiality

The interdisciplinary review of cases raises questions regarding the confidentiality of both ongoing police investigations and clinical interviews. The purpose of sharing information between police officers and clinicians is to deepen the team's understanding of children's experience of violence and to develop and implement coordinated interventions that address the needs of children and their families (see chapter 4). In their presentations of incidents which lead to referral to the CD-CP program, officers should not be expected to describe details of ongoing investigations. Similarly, clinical presentations should focus on the assessment of the impact of exposure to violence on the child's functioning and on information relevant to the development of a collaborative intervention plan. Further details of clinical treatment are confidential and should not be reported without permission.

### Case Review Process

The following principles can be applied to the task of assessing the adequacy and appropriateness of the plan of care developed at the conference:

- services should be informed by an understanding of the child's basic psychological, developmental, medical, and educational needs in the context of the child's history and life experiences;
- care must include working alliances among the child, the parents, police officers, and clinicians which are understood and maintained;
- services must be sufficiently flexible to be responsive to the changing needs of child and family and sustained for as long as child and family have need for them;
- plans for care must reflect a consensus of both police officers and clinicians present at the meeting.

#### INTEGRATION AND APPLICATION

In addition to the case management and planning purposes, the program conference provides an opportunity to discuss situations and events in the broader context of police and clinical activity. Issues that can be addressed beneficially include:

- the effects that services have on the actual care of specific children;
- the inferences that can be made from that information about the effectiveness of the overall program;
- the effect of the work on both police officers and clinicians;
- the application of mental health principles and strategies to other aspects of police work; and
- the integration of police knowledge and experience of communities and neighborhoods to the clinical understanding of children and families.

### SYSTEMIC AND INSTITUTIONAL ISSUES

The identification of barriers, disagreements, or problems within the program or with one of the collaborating institutions that affect the ability of the Child Development–Community Policing Program to meet its goals needs to be addressed regularly by the collaborators. The conference should provide a safe and *confidential* forum for the discussion of such systems issues. This process fosters group cohesion, increases the opportunities for mutual understanding of both the problems and the strengths that exist in police and mental health institutions, engenders mutual trust and respect, and supports the challenge of working with children and adolescents who are confronted by violence and traumatic stress.

Examples of this type of discussion include considering the psychological effect on both the children whose homes are forcibly entered by police during a drug raid and the police officers who participate in the raid, developing effective responses to officers who have been present at scenes where children have been brutally attacked, devising strategies to deal with a neighborhood group of young adolescents engaged in delinquent activity or community disorder, and coordinating the response to major incidents or community crises involving children with other institutions.

**ADMINISTRATION**

From time to time, the conference may assume an administrative and management function for the CD-CP program, handling such housekeeping details as identifying those who are in need of training, scheduling training sessions and other meetings, setting agendas, and dealing with budgetary and personnel matters within its purview. In addition, the program conference advocates and recommends policy and procedural changes to the respective institutions.

STEVEN NAGLER
STEVEN MARANS
MIRIAM BERKMAN
MARK SCHAEFER

# 6   Program Development

The Child Development–Community Policing Program is a collaborative effort between the police department and a child mental health agency of a particular community. As such, the relationships between the institutions and individuals within the institutions are the crucial factors in program development. Both the philosophy and the elements of the program have emphasized the importance of these relationships. This section offers a model for a program development process that is consistent with these principles. The collaborative process follows an interactive strategy that can guide a specific community's program development effort.

While each community's program will evolve in a unique way, it is recommended that key organizers of new programs consult with and receive technical assistance from the New Haven CD-CP program staff, so that the experience gained in New Haven can be communicated most effectively.

### PHASE 1: INSTITUTIONAL INVESTMENT

Because the CD-CP program's aim is fundamental change in the operations and the climate of the police department and mental health agency involved in the partnership, the leadership of both institutions must have a shared vision and commitment to the program. A meeting among the chief of police, the director of the collaborating mental health agency, and the chief executive (or designate) of the municipality is a critical first step in the process. Such a meeting, which may be convened by any one of the principals and may employ a consultant from the New Haven CD-CP Program, will set the parameters for the collaboration. Issues of time, money, staffing, program expectations, and evaluation need to be addressed at the outset. After these issues have been resolved by this group, the project is ready to move into the second phase of development.

### PHASE 2: INITIAL PROGRAM DEVELOPMENT

After the heads of the agencies have agreed on the broad goals and outline of the program, the field leadership of each institution can begin to develop the CD-CP model. A small working group forms the nucleus of the program. Depending on the size and scope of the program, three to five police officers and an equal number of mental health clinicians selected by their respective institutions serve as the key development and operations personnel.

They will be identified as Child Development–Community Policing fellows. In order to offer the leadership that a new program requires, it is recommended that the police officers be field supervisors (sergeants in most police departments), and that the mental health clinicians be their counterparts (usually program supervisors).

These six to ten individuals spend approximately a week together away from their regular responsibilities, training and preparing for the inception of the program. This immersion approach addresses the need for a shared body of knowledge and experience upon which the CD-CP program is based. It also begins the process of developing mutual respect and trust that is necessary for the program to flourish. The format of this week is a series of seminars and field experiences led by a team of a CD-CP experienced mental health clinician and police officer. The first half of the week is used for the seminars, site visits, and field observations. The second half of the week is devoted to planning by the CD-CP fellows for their own community, with the New Haven faculty as consultants and resource persons.

In previous program development seminars for the CD-CP program and other similar programs, it has proven useful for the field leadership to attend specifically designed training led by experienced CD-CP faculty. Such training should include:

- at least one full day of child and family development training with police officers and clinicians from New Haven;
- specifically arranged site visits to clinics and hospital units and discussion with clinicians who have clinical experience with CD-CP referrals;
- field observation with police officers with CD-CP experience;
- mental health and police counterparts serving as mentors; and

- seminar-format group discussion of officer training curricula, program elements, practical planning requirements, and location-specific considerations.

### PHASE 3: IMPLEMENTATION

Following the week of training, the fellows start initial clinical collaboration and curriculum and protocol planning, as well as fellowship activities and clinical referrals. The program conference also begins, focusing first on developing curricula for department-wide training and formal protocols for handling clinical cases. CD-CP program consultants from New Haven should remain available for consultation by telephone, fax, and mail.

At the end of one to three months, the curriculum and protocols should be developed and ready for dissemination and implementation. At this time it is helpful for the CD-CP consultants to visit the site and offer feedback and further guidance. The CD-CP program conference should from now on serve as the implementation and management vehicle for the program. Ongoing evaluation and program adjustments can be made in that forum.

### DATA AND RECORDS

As the CD-CP program develops, records of program activities will prove useful as a source of data for program adjustment, staff deployment, and planning additional, unanticipated program elements. They will also serve as a basis for reporting program activities to the responsible agencies and funding sources. The following activities should be recorded:

- number of case consultations;
- referrals accepted by families;
- referrals refused by families;

- officer or clinician consultations without referral;
- number of contacts between clinicians and child and/or family;
- number of contacts between officer and child and/or family; and
- number of interagency case discussions.

The CD-CP program also offers research opportunities for which this data will also be useful. Efforts by the Yale Child Study Center and the police departments of New Haven, Connecticut, and Framingham, Massachusetts, to measure the attitudes and expectations of police officers before and after CD-CP implementation are under way. New programs are encouraged to contact the Child Study Center to participate in these and other CD-CP research activities. (The appendix contains introductory report and case log forms used in New Haven to record descriptive clinical data and number of contacts.)

### BUDGETARY CONSIDERATIONS

Funding requirements are likely to vary considerably for different CD-CP programs, depending on the size of the community, the number of officers and clinicians involved in the program, and the design of the collaboration. These general considerations with regard to funding will be relevant to most communities.

The CD-CP program requires one senior clinician and one senior police officer to assume overall responsibility for leadership and coordination of the program. Depending on the scope and organization of the program being developed, both collaborating institutions must allocate resources to support the leadership activities of the coordinators.

The most significant expense associated with the CD-CP

program is the cost of training for police officers. This expense occurs primarily during the initial period of the program's operation, when large numbers of veteran officers participate in the training seminars. Ongoing operation of the program can be maintained with a lower level of funding. Depending on the size of the police force to be trained, the initial investment in officer training can be spread over several years, if necessary. It is important, however, that program planners have the funding necessary to train the entire department, and that at the outset officers are aware of a reasonable schedule for completing the process.

The cost of each training seminar consists of salary support for seminar leaders — a police supervisor and a clinician — for two hours per week for eight to ten weeks, and salary support for rank-and-file officers attending the seminar — ten to fifteen officers, two hours per week for eight to ten weeks. Officers may be assigned to the training seminar either in addition to or in lieu of other police duty. The cost of their attendance will therefore be borne either in extra pay for officers or in reduction of police presence on the street. It is not advisable to decrease the cost of officer training by increasing the size of the seminar classes because small group size is essential to the interactive nature of the seminar. Program planners are also advised not to decrease the expense of training by limiting seminar participation to selected members of the police force. Failure to offer the training seminar to all officers (or all interested officers) may lead to frustration and resentment within the police department, to the detriment of the CD-CP program.

The primary cost of the CD-CP fellowship is salary support for supervisory officers to attend clinical rotations and related discussions. As a guideline, fellowship activities have been scheduled in New Haven approximately three hours per week for three to four months, and four police fellows have participated at a time. As in the case of rank-and-file training, police departments have some flexibility to pay for this component of the program in extra pay for supervisors or in reduced supervision on the street. In New Haven, costs have been reduced by scheduling meetings during periods during which there typically are fewer calls for police service. In addition, officers on duty are always reachable by beeper or radio should they need to respond to a call immediately. The fellowship requires some salary support for clinical faculty; however, many rotations consist of observations at meetings or evaluations that will take place whether or not the fellows are present, and therefore do not require additional payment for faculty time.

The program conference may require some funding support for one and one-half to two hours per week for police supervisors and clinical personnel involved in the program — three to four officers and three to four clinicians at the beginning, and an expanding number of participants as the program grows. The costs of the program conference can be kept to a minimum by scheduling meetings at times of decreased police activity, rotating the time of meetings among shifts, and allowing supervisors attending the meeting to respond to calls for assistance and consultation from officers in the field. It is important that officers who have completed the fellowship training be offered an opportunity to remain involved in the weekly conference.

The consultation service requires partial salary support for several clinicians, who consult with police officers and provide clinical assessments and crisis intervention to children and families. The consultation service does not require funding for ongoing clinical treatment because public benefits, private insurance, and/or out-of-pocket payment should be available, as for any treatment provided by the collaborating mental health agency. The consultation service also does not require additional funding for the police because officers' responses to calls generally occur in the course of their regular police duties. Initially, the funding specifically required by the consultation service will be relatively modest, as relatively few referrals will be expected because relatively few officers will be trained and experienced in using the collaborative service. As calls to the consultation service increase, more clinical time will be required for emergency response, nonemergency response, clinical coordination, and tracking of referrals.

Much of the work of the CD-CP program does not require additional funding for the police department or collaborating mental health agency, but, rather, requires a shift in both agencies' deployment of existing personnel. For example, the program encourages officers to make frequent follow-up visits to the homes of children and families who were victims or witnesses of violence. If the program is to be successful, this sort of work must be considered part of routine patrol, not extra duty requiring separate funding. Similarly, the program requires a shift of some clinical resources from traditional, clinic-based practice to home visits and emergency call. However, in New Haven this shift has not incurred any dramatic increases in clinical costs. Home visits and emergency contact have not only been indicated in many cases, but also have decreased the number of costly empty hours that would have been created by no-shows or canceled appointments made for outpatient clinics.

# 7 Results of the New Haven Program

The Child Development–Community Policing Program has been in operation in New Haven since January 1992. During the first three years, the program has trained all four hundred and fifty members of the New Haven police force in the use of the consultation service; one hundred and sixty officers have completed the seminars on child development and human functioning; twenty-five police supervisors (sergeants and lieutenants) and the assistant chief of police have completed the fellowship and continue to meet with Child Study Center faculty in the weekly program conference. Six police supervisors have joined with the clinical faculty to staff the consultation service.

During the first three years, the consultation service has received more than two hundred calls from officers in the field regarding more than four hundred and fifty children, ranging in age from two to seventeen years old. The children have been involved in violent events in their homes and in the community; they have been involved as victims, as witnesses, and as perpetrators. They have been exposed to murders, stabbings, beatings, robberies, gunfire, maiming by fire, death by drowning, kidnapping, traffic accidents, and attempted and completed suicides. Other children not exposed to acute episodes of violence have also been referred to the consultation service by officers who knew the children well enough to have concerns about their emotional well-being or about worsening behavior which was not yet criminal. Through the consultation service, initial clinical contact occurs from within minutes of a violent event to several days later when immediate attention is not indicated or is declined. In most cases, children have been seen individually. In cases in which large groups of children were exposed to an episode of violence or a tragedy, children and their parents were seen in groups. Children have been seen in their homes, in police stations, at the Child Study Center, in hospitals, and in other community settings.

## CHANGES IN POLICE PRACTICE

### Trauma, Police, and Mental Health

The CD-CP program was initiated with the aim of establishing a broader psychological safety net for children and families who had witnessed violence in their homes and on their streets. It was thought that because police officers are most frequently involved with these families, they are well-placed for providing outreach and making referrals for clinical services. However, as police and mental health professionals spent increasing amounts of time with each other and with victims of violent crimes, their appreciation of the experience and meaning of chronic exposure to violence and the potential for traumatization grew. Familiar notions about trauma and the need to guard against feeling overwhelmed — through avoidance of feelings and subsequent development of symptoms that interfere with optimal functioning — applied as much to the professionals responding to the scenes of violence as they did to the children and families (Marans, Berkman, and Cohen, in press).

Responses to calls involving domestic violence, homicides, robberies, gang- and drug-related activities, civil disturbances, and the like, make officers especially vulnerable to chronic exposure to disturbing scenes of violence. Especially when children are involved, police officers often leave these scenes overwhelmed, frustrated, and unlikely to pay attention to the emotional response of children. Furthermore, the police have no options for intervening on their behalf. Officers defend against their own feelings of helplessness and despair in their identification with the children and against the fear they experience on a regular basis about the danger that may await them at the next call for service. They remain anonymous, distant, and perfunctory, turning away from suffering of children, or feel rage and disdain for the adults who have exposed them to terror.

Police officers' previous exposure to mental health professionals had been limited to delivering psychotic patients to the emergency room or waiting hours for protective services workers to respond to a request to remove a battered or grossly neglected child from the home. For many police officers, mental health and social service professionals had frequently been viewed as armchair or consulting room apologists for behavior that officers would clearly define as wrong, not "disturbed." Initially, many rank-and-file officers felt that the department was asking them to change their professional identities from that of cop to social worker. It became evident that many officers felt that the notion of becoming more sensitive to the plight of the subjects of their investigations and encounters was tantamount to inviting a breach in necessary strategies for coping with the stress of confronting human tragedy on a regular basis. If the potential role of officers responding to children at scenes of violence was to expand, this would not happen by memo alone. Police officers would need to add to their repertoire of knowledge, interventions, and backup support.

### Practice and Procedures

The experience in New Haven has made it clear that officers need to have support for their expanded role at many levels. As part of the Child Development–Community Policing Program, the changes in practice and support include:

- relatively stable assignment to a specific district in order to develop and sustain relationships with community members;
- protocols and supervision that establish a standard of involvement with children and families at scenes of violent crimes (including offering immediate and follow-up clinical consultation with mental health colleagues as well as follow-up contact by the officer after the event);
- training in basic principles of child development and human functioning relevant to policing strategies;
- availability and use of immediate and follow-up consultation with mental health colleagues on a twenty-four-hour basis regarding all acute episodes of violence involving children as well as concerns about at-risk and delinquent behavior;
- ongoing contact between mental health colleagues and police officers about clinical referrals and coordination of services and activities, program development, as well as

opportunities to discuss the emotional and strategic responses of police and mental health professionals in specific cases;

- ongoing discussion of the collaborative process at the institutional and administrative level;
- increased contact among officers, school personnel, clergy, and social services and community leaders regarding concerns about violence, gang-related disputes, and civil disturbances brokered by policing supervisors and mental health colleagues;
- review of cases involving juvenile offenders by police and mental health collaborators in order to provide more immediate access to treatment interventions where appropriate; and
- follow-up and assessment of need for clinical intervention for any children who witness drug raids carried out by narcotics officers.

### New Roles for Officers

In addition to these departmental changes in practice, officers report that the multiple facets of the program make them feel more effective in their work on the street, particularly in dealing with the tragedy of violence. When they are not the only professionals contending with the aftermath of violence and when they attend to the emotional needs of children and families and deliver direct services, officers feel that they have a new way of "taking control" of highly disturbing situations. Rather than becoming overwhelmed, sealing over, and turning away from these scenes, officers assume active roles as benign figures of authority who help to reestablish a semblance of stability in the midst of the emotional chaos that so often characterizes the lives of children and families who in the past have had to bear the burden of community violence on their own. In addition, officers report, as they have assumed supportive roles in the lives of children and families, they are better able to establish positive, trusting relationships which are likely to be valuable in pursuing law enforcement goals in the community. For officers in New Haven, the CD-CP program has not only opened up a new and unique partnership with mental health professionals, but it has also helped pave the way for a new relationship with members of the community.

## CHANGES IN CLINICAL PRACTICE

### House Calls

As a result of the CD-CP program, children and families who would not previously have been seen at the Child Study Center have been referred for treatment. Engagement with these families has required clinicians to leave their consulting rooms and go into the community, make the hours of their work more flexible in order to respond immediately to incidents of violence involving children, and eliminate potential procedural barriers to service. Many of the families referred through the consultation service have been initially distrustful and reluctant to use mental health services, or have experienced formidable obstacles to obtaining service (lack of financial resources, transportation, or day care for other children in the family). Unlike traditional practice of offering office appointments, initial contacts with many of these families have taken place at home, and, when ongoing treatment has been recommended for many of these children, clinicians have taken a much more active role in facilitating the family's transfer to a clinic-based treatment (by arranging transportation, personally introducing the clinic-based therapist, making follow-up telephone calls, and so on) or have maintained longer term home-based interventions.

For many families coping with acute and chronic episodes of community violence, less active outreach and support resulted in incomplete referrals and/or aborted treatment.

In addition, for many of the children and families seen through the consultation service, the referrals may offer not only accessible and responsive clinical service for the first time, but also may reflect a new and different experience with police officers. Regardless of the outcome of the clinical referral, follow-up visits allow officers to support adult caregivers in responding to their children's distress, as well as to reinforce the child's view that the officer is a source of concern and safety and a potential role model. In fact, officers' follow-up visits to children and families exposed to violence have at times been *the* crucial factor in the rate of recovery and psychological reorganization.

### Police as Partners

Through the CD-CP program, clinicians have also learned to collaborate with police officers as part of their clinical work. Prior to the inception of the program, clinicians would not have thought of the police as a likely source of information about a child's history, adult support and guidance for a troubled youth, or stability and safety for a parent having difficulty meeting her or his children's needs in the wake of her or his own traumatization. Experience in the CD-CP program has taught clinicians to see the police department as a valuable community resource and to call upon officers for support in work with children and families, as they would call on other professionals in the community like teachers, clergy, or youth activity leaders.

In addition, the CD-CP program has exposed mental health professionals to the intimate details of children's experience of violence and life in the inner city in ways that would not have been possible through more traditional clinical practice. When clinicians venture out to scenes of violent incidents, when they spend time with officers learning about specific neighborhoods, they can better understand the events and circumstances that the children they treat have experienced, and, as a consequence, they can more clearly analyze the children's reactions and patterns of adaptation.

## CLINICAL FINDINGS

### Violence and Traumatization

Similar to the findings of other investigators (Terr, 1989, 1991; Pynoos and Nader, 1988, 1989, 1990), our observations suggest that the degree of a child's disturbance or traumatization is determined by an interplay of factors within the child and in his surroundings:

- characteristics of the violence itself (the child's relationship to the perpetrator and victim, proximity to the incident, response of the caregivers);
- the developmental phase of the child (the emotional and cognitive resources available for mediating anxiety associated with objective and fantasized dangers);
- the familial and community context of the violent incident (isolated and unusual or part of a chronic pattern of experience of daily life); and
- ability of family members, school personnel, and community institutions to recognize and provide sustained responses to the possible effects of the child's exposure to violence.

In addition, although there is tremendous variation among children seen by the consultation service clinicians and police officers, some commonly reported observations include:

- disbelief and denial of the outcome of the violent event;
- intense longing and concern about the presence, safety, and well-being of family members, even when they are not involved in any aspect of the violent incident;
- reviving and much talking about previous losses, injuries, fights, and other episodes of violence;
- retelling the events with alterations of the facts that would lead to different outcomes, described by Pynoos as "intervention fantasies" (R. S. Pynoos, personal communication);
- attributing blame to those not directly involved in the violence; and
- reveling in the excitement of the violent action with talk of the weapons used and who got "capped," "smoked," or "aired" (Marans, 1994).

### Phase Development, Trauma, and Interventions

Referrals from the CD-CP consultation service have demonstrated impressively the extent to which children describe the violent events they have witnessed in terms of the developmental phase–specific anxieties. In the unfolding stories of the children exposed to violence, we can see clearly what constitutes the specific danger that overwhelms the individual child, or what aspects and meanings of the event are experienced as exceptional, overwhelming, and therefore "traumatizing." All too often, clinical assumptions about the nature of a child's traumatization seem to be determined by the facts about the violence that has been witnessed and may have little to do with the child's experience of the event or the meaning attributed by the child in its aftermath. In turn, there may be little attention paid to learning about the child in order to begin to appreciate what an experience of violence might be for the individual child in the context of his or her life and, therefore, what interventions could be most useful. Greater awareness of the specificity of individual children's concerns and the ways in which these concerns define traumatization has direct implications for clinical work, as well as informing immediate and follow-up strategies for intervening in the community and with those institutions involved in the life of children and their families.

## CASE ILLUSTRATIONS

### A Shooting on a School Bus: Acute Response

At midday on a late spring day, a school bus bearing eight five- and six-year-olds was caught in the cross fire of rival drug dealers. Several bullets hit the bus; a six-year-old boy was shot in the head. The bus went to a nearby middle school where the children were met by police officers and emergency medical personnel. The boy who was shot was taken to the hospital. He survived surgery and suffered some neurological impairment for which he received long-term rehabilitation. Officers trained in the CD-CP program were the first to meet the children and contacted members of the consultation service to come to the middle school. The uninjured children were taken inside the middle school building by police officers, who immediately began coordinating efforts to get parents of each child to the middle school. The officers described their central aim as protecting the children from the excitement surrounding the shooting — camera crews, multiple police personnel, onlookers — and securing the most immediate source of comfort possible by reuniting them with parents. Children were *not* interviewed by officers about the shooting; officers explained that, while in the past this would have been part of the standard investigation, any information about the shooting police might get from the children was not immediately necessary and, as the police supervisor on the scene noted, "would only re-traumatize the children, especially when what they needed the most was to be with their parents."

The CD-CP clinicians arrived on the scene within ten minutes of the shooting. They were briefed by police colleagues already at the middle school and were taken to the gym where the seven children were sitting on the floor. Middle school personnel attempted to engage the children in a discussion about what they had seen, but the children remained quiet, clutching their knees and staring into the middle distance. The CD-CP clinicians were introduced to the school personnel, who moved to the background as the clinicians began to work with the children. The clinicians had brought paper and markers. They sat down with two children each, asking one child, then the other, if he or she would like to draw a picture. Each child quietly declined, but, when asked if they would like the clinician to draw something, the positive response was unanimous, as was the requested content of the pictures: "Draw my mommy." Each child was asked what sort of face the mommy should have and what words might fill the speech bubble next to the drawing of the face. The instructions for faces fell in two categories: happy and sad. The words conveyed either "I'm so happy to see you" or "I was so sad and worried about you." After engaging in the drawings, the children grew more verbal and began to make inquiries about where their mothers were and when they would arrive. All the children also expressed concern that perhaps their mothers had been hurt and might not be coming for them. The senior police officer on the scene, a CD-CP fellow, told the children and clinicians that all the parents had been located and were on the way to the school.

One of the children asked a clinician to draw a picture of a head. Whose head? "Um, a boy's head . . . that just got shot with a bullet." The rest of the children overheard this question and immediately turned their attention to the picture. The clinician requested details in order to complete the picture and asked if any of the children wished to add something. Three children scribbled the same ingredient with a red marker—blood from the head wound—that soon covered much of the page. Although there were some questions about what was happening to the friend who had been shot, the majority of questions and comments had to do with bodily functions (How much blood does the body have? Can parts of the body fall off?) and quickly turned to a more spirited group discussion about various physical feats each child could perform. The discussion continued to be punctuated by the children's sidelong glances toward the door as parents began to arrive to pick up their children. Each parent was seen briefly by the clinician, and all were given a telephone number to call at any time with questions regarding their children's experiences, and asked if they could be contacted for follow-up assessments.

While the crime scene was secured and the criminal investigation begun, attention was paid to the emotional needs of all the children who were caught up in the experience of violence. The Child Development–Community Policing Program, in conjunction with the school system, coordinated and carried out all aspects of the response to the shooting, including informing both the middle school and elementary school communities about the shooting, briefing parents and school personnel, consulting with teachers, school administrators, and parents about how to respond to children in the classroom and at home, and making additional clinical services available. Police officers trained in the program were able to give out information about the shooting in formal briefing sessions with parents and school personnel and in informal encounters with the children who approached them in the streets. They explained the circumstances and background of the shooting, as well as understanding the adults' rage and feelings of helplessness, in an effective and sensitive manner that indicated their sophistication about the complexity of responses of individuals exposed to violence.

The CD-CP officers and clinicians were also able to influence community responses to the shooting. They successfully argued that, although it might make some adults feel less helpless, escorting school buses with squad cars the day after the shooting would only exacerbate children's concerns about safety. In a similar vein, with greater appreciation for children's anxiety and vulnerability, officers discussed their concerns about the children as they kept at bay the media who gathered around the children's school soon after the shooting and in the days that followed. Their intervention minimized the intrusiveness and associated excitement of cameras and of reporters asking children and families a barrage of questions. As a consequence of the CD-CP responses to the shooting incident, the police were seen not merely as the harbingers of tragic news and violence but as sources of effective authority, concerned about the safety and emotional well-being of the affected children and families.

### Clinical Follow-up

Five of the seven children received brief follow-up psychotherapy because of enduring post-traumatic stress symptoms — disruptions in sleeping and eating; increased separation anxiety; and hypervigilance, generalized anxiety, and avoidant behaviors that were not part of the premorbid history. Two vignettes offer illustrations of the ways in which developmental phase and individual circumstances determine the context and specific meaning given to the disturbing external event. Each case example represents a condensation of material that emerged over the course of two to four months of treatment once and twice a week.

*Beverly*  Beverly, five and a half years old, was sitting on the bus across the aisle from her classmate when he was shot (all names in this chapter have ben changed). Her previous school functioning was good, as was her adaptation in an intact family that included her mother, father, and a ten-month-old brother. Her developmental history was unremarkable. After the shooting, Beverly's difficulties with sleeping and eating, multiple new fears, and need to remain close to her mother continued unabated for two weeks before her parents agreed with the clinician's recommendation for individual work with the child in conjunction with parent guidance.

In her individual sessions, Beverly repeatedly returned to the shooting, reviewing an increasing array of details in both play with toy figures and in her drawings. Each narrative ended with Beverly stating that she felt scared or "bad." Over time, the therapist probed these feelings further, within either the action of the play or the narrative that accompanied the pictures. Beverly elaborated that she felt scared that the bullet could have hit her and felt bad because her friend had been hurt. In one session, she drew a picture of herself and her friend on the bus. She drew the bullet tracking around her head on an eventual path to the head of her classmate. She grew quiet and looked forlorn. With the suggestion that there was a connection between her feelings and the story that lay behind the picture, Beverly revealed a secret whose telling spanned many sessions and was accompanied by a dramatic reduction and final resolution of her presenting symptoms.

The first part of the secret was that, for several days before the shooting, Beverly had been reprimanded by the driver for bad behavior on the bus. Beverly thought that perhaps the bullet had been meant for her as punishment. Later, she told the therapist that her "bad" behavior had been about her teasing and poking at the classmate who was shot. The third part of the secret was about her baby brother. With great anxiety, Beverly reported that she teased the baby on numerous occasions and that she often wished that her brother were no longer around. With this, the sources of her worry and guilt became more clear. She was able to articulate her fear that somehow her bad wishes about her pesky brother had come true in the shooting of her schoolmate and that her wishes would be discovered and severely punished. The therapist was able to point out that Beverly was punishing herself as if the reality of the scary events had somehow been under her magical control. Beverly's hostile wishes toward a rival baby brother and their displacement onto a schoolmate was not unusual. For Beverly, however, the *realization* of these wishes — if only in the displacement — constituted the central source of her overwhelming anxiety and traumatization. In addition, her sense of magical control reflected both age-expectable phenomena augmented by reliance on magic for the purposes of restitution and recovery. That is, a belief in magical control revised the original experience of traumatization, or absence of control, in the shooting — even if the belief in magic might also lead to a tremendous sense of responsibility for and guilt about the real and imagined events.

*Miguel* Miguel, five years old, presented with multiple symptoms. He was the youngest in a family of six. Both parents and a nineteen-year-old brother worked, one sister was in high school, and the other was in middle school. Prior to the shooting of his classmate, Miguel had had no difficulty sleeping, leaving home for school, or engaging in activities away from home. This changed dramatically after the incident on the school bus. He insisted on sleeping with the light on at night, departures from home were very upsetting for him, and in the remaining days of school he complained of sickness in order to avoid going. After several weeks of treatment Miguel revealed in his play that he was terrified that the people responsible for the shooting of his classmate would come to shoot him and all his family. The fact that the shooters had been arrested and were in jail did not alleviate Miguel's fears or symptoms. However, his ability to express this central worry opened the door for further exploration, clarification of his thoughts, and greater mastery over a very frightening experience.

What lay behind Miguel's fear of being shot was his attempt to explain to himself why the shooting had happened and, perhaps, with this explanation he felt more able to predict similarly dangerous events. However, the explanation Miguel developed was limited by the condensation and concrete thinking typical of his phase of development. Miguel eventually explained the following ideas to his therapist and then to his parents. He had learned in school about how bad drugs are and that, in addition to the terrible things they do to the body, they make people violent and are the cause of fights between drug dealers. When the shooting started and the bus was hit by gunfire, Miguel assumed that the shooting was about drugs and, if the school bus was being shot at, it must somehow be involved with drugs. If the school bus was involved in drugs and he was on the school bus, then he must somehow be connected with drugs. If he was involved in drugs, then so must his family. If he and the family were involved in drugs, they would fall victim to gunfire just like his classmate. Although there was no indication that the family was involved in drug use or dealing, the dangers were brought home to Miguel as a powerful response to being shot at and seeing blood flow from his friend's head wound. While generating considerable fear, Miguel's explanation relied on the cognitive resources available to him and provided the basis for altering the traumatic episode. In his version, Miguel was able to anticipate the danger — he expected assailants to come after him — and he defended against the danger — he remained hypervigilant (staying up at night, staying close to home, keeping family nearby). Understanding Miguel's solution in the context of phase-specific concerns and capacities helped Miguel to unravel and clarify the distinction between his fantasy configurations and the factual information and led to a resolution of his developmental crisis and the attendant symptoms.

Where phase-appropriate concerns associated with the body and sibling rivalry, magical and concrete thinking played a crucial role in understanding and addressing the nature of trauma for Beverly and Miguel, respectively, another incident illustrated an adolescent version of overwhelming, disorganizing anxiety.

### An Adolescent Victim

Mark, aged fifteen, was robbed at gunpoint on a Friday evening. He had been walking with friends when two men pointed what Mark said was a large caliber semiautomatic weapon in his face and demanded all his money and jewelry. Mark had been walking behind several friends, and they were unaware of what was occurring in an alley off the sidewalk. Mark later reported that the men repeatedly shoved the weapon in his face and told him they would shoot him. After taking his valuables, the assailants fled and Mark ran home. He ran into his room crying uncontrollably, hid on the floor of his closet, and, in spite of his mother's urging, refused to come out. After a while, a sobbing Mark told his mother what had occurred and she telephoned the police. All three officers who arrived had been trained in the child development seminars, and the supervisory officer had completed the fellowship. As one of the officers approached the bedroom, Mark began to scream. The officer told him that he had heard what had happened and realized that the holdup was a terrifying experience. Mark would not look at the officer and yelled at him to leave the room. The officer was about to leave when the supervisor pointed to his gun and utility belt. The officer removed his holster and weapon, explaining to Mark that he would leave them outside the room, as he understood how frightening guns might be to Mark, who continued to sob and shake uncontrollably. Mark allowed the officer to help him out of the room and accepted the suggestion that he go to the emergency room for treatment. The consultation service clinician was called and met Mark at the hospital.

During the course of the interview, Mark was only able to look at the clinician after a comment was made about how feeling very frightened could make a guy feel small and helpless — a very undesirable feeling for a fifteen-year-old. Mark began to talk about the events, recounting the same scene and assailants' commands to him over and over. The repetition began to include some slight alterations in the facts, and Mark protested that he should have "grabbed the gun and kicked each of the [attackers] in the balls." He described the gun muzzle as huge and insisted that he thought they would kill him with this large weapon. As his shaking, hyperventilating, and sobbing subsided, Mark began to talk about the earlier part of the evening. He explained that before being robbed he had been "hanging back from [his] homeboys because they were with their ladies" and he wanted to "give them space." He shyly told the clinician that he did not have a girlfriend and quickly exploded with rage and then tears. He wanted to get a gun and kill the guys who "messed with him." He did not deserve what had happened to him — he was a good student in school and had just completed an important history paper. He explained that he had bought all the thin gold chains he had been wearing — clarifying that he was not to be lumped together with what he called "low-life drug dealers." Mark began to cry again as he swore revenge. The clinician commented that it must have been humiliating to feel so terrified and that Mark must be wishing that he could undo his experience. Mark replied that if he had a gun or had disarmed his attackers, he would not feel as though he'd "wimped out." The clinician agreed that feeling powerful would certainly be the opposite of what he had experienced with a gun in his face. Mark's expression brightened and he looked up, exclaiming that now he remembered the gun more clearly — it had not been a 9 mm. semi-automatic, but a BB gun. As his acute terror diminished, he was also able to remember the make of the car the muggers drove off in as well as clear descriptions of the two men. His restitution fantasies of revenge began to take another form as Mark talked about helping the police make an arrest. Mark asked to speak with the detective involved in the case to offer the information he had recovered in the course of the interview with the clinician. Two hours after the admission to the emergency room, Mark was discharged.

Mark was seen in two follow-up sessions in which he continued to go over the events. The fantasies of what he should have done were intermingled with talk of the mortification of feeling helpless and the increasing recognition that there was nothing he could have done to alter what had occurred. When his sleeping difficulties and hypervigilant feelings abated, Mark declined further clinical contact. However, over the following several weeks one of the responding officers stopped by regularly for brief chats during the course of their usual patrol. In the last clinical follow-up, eight weeks after the incident, Mark had still not bought a gun, and, instead of reciting numerous violent revenge fantasies, he spoke of the latest academic demands at school and of his new friendships with the cops on his beat. While he had not forgotten the terror or rage associated with his experience, Mark added that his good memory had been instrumental in helping the police to arrest the two men who had attacked him — "That felt really good."

## DISCUSSION

Although our findings are preliminary, two groups of children exposed to violence seem most vulnerable to longer term presentation of affective, attentional, and behavioral difficulties. Not surprisingly, one group includes children whose development had already appeared compromised and who were symptomatic prior to witnessing a violent event. The second group of children includes those whose initial responses are quiet and unobtrusive to the adult caregivers — or whose gross symptomatology is not seen by caregivers as causally linked to the child's exposure to a disturbing scene of violence. When children are unable to understand, let alone directly verbalize, their traumatic experiences, adults are often unable to interpret children's actions or listen to symptomatic language that communicates distress. In addition, adults are by no means immune to feelings of overwhelming helplessness and fear that accompany their own experiences of the violence in their homes and neighborhoods. Their own inability to listen and to attend to their children's needs may be a natural consequence of their own attempts at restitution and self-protection from the feelings of vulnerability. The wish to push away upsetting images and feelings is especially powerful when the events that evoked them are so dangerous and real.

These phenomena have a special bearing on health care providers and police officers as well. By personal disposition and training, police officers and mental health professionals are called upon (and call upon themselves) to treat *actively* and cure the ills of patients or to "serve and protect" citizens to the best of their abilities and resources. In cases involving children who have witnessed incidents of violence, the urge to act — and the wish to make things better quickly — may be a way of dealing with the same anxiety and feelings of helplessness that the children and their families experience. However, the sense of urgency at these moments may interfere with the most significant, initial intervention — to listen, to attend, and then to act.

The Child Development–Community Policing Program has

created a relationship between professionals who have long been concerned about the spiraling incidence of violence and antisocial behavior but until now have worked separately — each profession lamenting the limitations of its traditional attempts to intervene and interrupt that cycle. In our collaboration, we have learned that the best police officers and the best clinicians share not only concerns about the most vulnerable members of society but the capacity to observe and learn from their observations. By joining forces, developing a common language for their experiences, and learning from one another, police and mental health professionals have expanded the ways in which they think and act on behalf of the children who are at the greatest risk of being traumatized by community violence and becoming the next generation of violent perpetrators.

# Appendix

**YALE CHILD STUDY CENTER POST-TRAUMATIC STRESS QUESTIONNAIRE PARENT FORM**

The following is a guide for an interview with parents of a child exposed to a violent incident. The questions are intended to follow collection of the general demographic data in the introductory report form.

If it's OK with you, I'd like to ask you a few questions about how [child's name] and the rest of your family are doing after [the incident].

### Part I. Child

(A)  In general, how is [child's name] doing now?

(B) Have you noticed any changes in [your child's] behavior or emotions since [the incident]? Describe.

(C) I am going to ask you some more specific questions about children's behavior and feelings, and it would be helpful if you would tell me if you have noticed any of these changes in [your child] since [the incident].

  1. Does [your child] have more difficulty sleeping? (Trouble falling asleep, sleeping through the night, sleeping in own bed, nightmares)
     Yes _____    No _____
     Describe:

  2. Have there been any changes in [your child's] eating habits? (Eating more, less, refusing to eat)
     Yes _____    No _____
     Describe:

  3. Has [your child] been more clingy or had more difficulty separating from you to go to school or other activities?
     Yes _____    No _____
     Describe:

  4. Has [your child] been more irritable, angry or had more trouble getting along with other people?
     Yes _____    No _____
     Describe:

  5. Has [your child] been more sad or tearful than usual?
     Yes _____    No _____
     Describe:

  6. Has [your child] been more easily excited, silly, or babyish?
     Yes _____    No _____
     Describe:

  7. Has [your child] been more quiet or withdrawn than usual?
     Yes _____    No _____
     Describe:

8. Has [your child] had more difficulty concentrating or paying attention?
   Yes _____        No _____
   Describe:

9. Have there been any changes in [your child's] play?
   Yes _____        No _____
   Describe:

10. Does [your child] think a lot about what happened or talk a lot about what happened?
    Yes _____        No _____
    Describe:

11. Has [your child] been more worried or fearful than usual? Is he or she afraid of specific things?
    Yes _____        No _____
    Describe:

12. Has [your child] had any illnesses since the incident?
    Yes _____        No _____
    Describe:

13. Has [your child] more cuts, scrapes, or bruises than usual?
    Yes _____        No _____
    Describe:

14. Does [your child] startle more easily than usual?
    Yes _____        No _____
    Describe:

15. Does [your child] have thoughts or pictures of what happened come into his or her mind? Even when he or she doesn't want them to?
    · Yes _____        No _____
    Describe:

16. Do certain things remind [your child] of [the event]? Does he or she try to avoid those things?

Yes _____    No _____

Describe:

(D)  Do you have any other concerns about your child?

## Part II. Parent and Family

In addition to [child's name], I am also interested in how you and other members of your family are doing. If it's OK, I would like to ask a few questions about you and the rest of the family.

(A)  In general, how have you been feeling?

(B)  Have you been thinking a lot about what happened?

Yes _____    No _____

Describe:

(C)  Have you noticed any changes in how you and other members of your family are getting along with each other?

Yes _____    No _____

Describe:

(D)  Have there been any changes in your sleeping patterns?

Yes _____    No _____

Describe:

(E)  Have there been any changes in your eating habits?

Yes _____    No _____

Describe:

(F)  Have you had more difficulty concentrating or paying attention?

Yes _____    No _____

Describe:

(G)  Have you been more sad or tearful than usual?

Yes _____    No _____

Describe:

(H) Have you been more worried or fearful than usual?
Yes _____      No _____
Describe:

(I)  What about other members of your family? Have you noticed any
of the changes in mood or behavior that we have been talking about
in any other member of your household?
Describe:

(J)  Do you have any other concerns about anyone in your family?

## CHILD DEVELOPMENT–COMMUNITY POLICING PROGRAM
## INTRODUCTORY REPORT

For research use:
Child ID#: _____
Event ID#: _____

*Directions:* The following report should be completed by the CD-CP clinician shortly after referral.

Today's date: _____ Date of referral: _____ Date of first contact: _____

Name of person referring: _____ Role in relationship to child: ___

Child's full name: _____ Gender: M [  ] F [  ]

Address: _____
Street        City        State        Zip        Phone

Date of Birth: _____ Age: ___ years ___ months

Race/ethnicity:
African-American [  ]   Hispanic        [  ]   Native American [  ]
Caucasian        [  ]   Asian-American  [  ]   Other            [  ]
                                               (specify: _____)

Religion:
Jewish [  ] Muslim [  ] Protestant [  ] Roman Catholic [  ] Other: _____

School: _____ Grade: ___ Special education? Yes [  ] No [  ]

Household members:

| First and last name | Sex | Age | Grade/occupation | Relationship to child |
|---|---|---|---|---|
|  |  |  |  |  |
|  |  |  |  |  |
|  |  |  |  |  |
|  |  |  |  |  |
|  |  |  |  |  |
|  |  |  |  |  |
|  |  |  |  |  |
|  |  |  |  |  |

How long has child been a member of current household? _____

Significant family members outside of child's home: _____

Please provide a brief description of traumatic event and child's or family's presenting difficulties:




### Descriptive Data

I.  Who referred the child? (Please check one.)
    A.  Patrol Officer
        1.  CD/CP graduate                          _____
        2.  Non CD/CP graduate                      _____
    B.  Supervisor
        1.  CD/CP Fellow                            _____
        2.  Non CD/CP Fellow                        _____
    C.  Detective
        1.  CD/CP                                   _____
        2.  Non CD/CP
    D.  Self-referred (CD/CP clinician)             _____
    E.  Other professional                          _____
    F.  Other (specify: _____)                   _____

II. What is the primary reason for CD/CP clinician involvement?
    (check all that apply)
    A.  Acute traumatic event       [ ]  (complete only section III)
    B.  Delinquent behavior         [ ]  (complete only section IV)
    C.  Psychiatric difficulties    [ ]  (complete only section V)
    D.  Family problems             [ ]  (complete only section VI)

III. Which of the following best categorize the nature of the call?
     (Please check all that apply.)
     A.  Beeper _____          Other _____
     B.  Response statistics: (please provide estimated statistics if uncertain)

| Marker | Date | Time (A.M./P.M.) |
|---|---|---|
| Event | | |
| Police notification | | |
| Police arrival | | |
| Clinician notification | | |
| Clinician arrival | | |

C. Context of event
   1. Domestic dispute    Yes _____ No _____
   2. Drug related    Yes _____ No _____
   3. Gang related    Yes _____ No _____
   4. Other _____
D. Nature of event
   1. murder                                                    _____
   2. physical assault (includes child abuse)    _____
   3. sexual assault                                         _____
   4. kidnapping                                            _____
   5. robbery                                                 _____
   6. accident                                                _____
      a. fire                                                    _____
      b. auto                                                  _____
      c. drowning                                           _____
      d. accidental shooting                            _____
      e. other (specify: _____)
   7. suicide attempt/completion                    _____
   8. civil disturbance (e.g., riot, gang related
      violence, etc.)                                         _____
   9. shooting/gunfire                                    _____
   10. drug raid                                             _____
   11. other aggressive police action
       (specify: _____)                              _____

E. Were weapons involved?
    1. gun                                                        _____
    2. knife                                                     _____
    3. blunt instrument (e.g., club, bat)     _____
    4. other (specify: _____)             _____
    5. no weapon                                    _____
F. Where did the event occur?
    1. home                                               _____
    2. school                                          _____
    3. community                                  _____

The following questions relate to those present at the scene of the event, at the time of the event. Do not include persons who appeared on the scene after the event.

G. How many immediate or extended family members and other significant figures in child's life were present at scene? (Do not include child.)           _____
H. Approximately how many other persons were present at scene?
    1. Children (Birth to 12)             _____
    2. Adolescents (13–17)             _____
    3. Adults (18 or older)             _____

Comments: _____

_____

_____

I. Please identify the outcome associated with each immediate or extended family member and other significant figures in the child's life including the child. Include only those present at the time of event and those who arrived during the police investigation. Categories are identified below table. Numbers may be used rather than labels.

| Relationship to child[a] | Role in event | Outcome | Reaction to event[b] |
|---|---|---|---|
| Child | | | |
| | | | |
| | | | |
| | | | |
| | | | |
| | | | |
| | | | |

[a]Please indicate primary attachment figure(s) with an asterisk (*) if present.
[b]Please indicate whether by observation (O) or by report (R).

Relationship to child
1. mother
2. father
3. step-mother (or equivalent)
4. step-father (or equivalent)
5. female relative caregiver
6. male relative caregiver
7. foster mother
8. foster father
9. other relative
10. brother
11. sister

Role in event
1. victim
2. perpetrator
3. witness/bystander
4. present, not direct witness to event
5. arrived after event

Outcome
1. fatal
2. non-fatal injury requiring overnight hospitalization
3. non-fatal injury requiring treatment by physician
4. non-fatal injury, treatment by physician not required
5. no injury
6. arrested, incarcerated
7. arrested, not incarcerated

Reaction to event
1. calm
2. quiet
3. detached
4. agitated
5. tearful/crying
6. staring
7. talkative
8. shivering/tremors
9. clinging
10. limp/unresponsive
11. unconscious
12. somatic complaints
13. oppositional
14. enraged/aggressive
15. hypermotoric
16. difficulty breathing
17. incontinent of urine
18. asleep

J.  Please identify relationship to child and outcome for every other person at the scene who was either a victim or perpetrator.

| Relationship to child | Role in event | Outcome |
|---|---|---|
|  |  |  |
|  |  |  |
|  |  |  |
|  |  |  |
|  |  |  |
|  |  |  |
|  |  |  |
|  |  |  |

Relationship to child
1. unfamiliar adult
2. familiar adult
3. unfamiliar adolescent
4. familiar adolescent
5. unfamiliar child
6. familiar child

Role in event
1. victim
2. perpetrator

Outcome
1. fatal
2. non-fatal injury requiring overnight hospitalization
3. non-fatal injury requiring treatment by physician
4. non-fatal injury, treatment by physician not required
5. no injury
6. arrested, incarcerated
7. arrested, not incarcerated

IV. Nature of delinquent behavior.
    A.    Involvement in statutory offenses.
        1. Alcohol use     _____
        2. Curfew violation     _____
        3. Run away     _____
        4. Other (specify: _____)     _____
    B.    Current involvement in criminal offenses.
        1. Drug possession     _____
        2. Drug dealing     _____
        3. Breaking and entering     _____
        4. Robbery (armed)     _____
        5. Robbery (unarmed)     _____
        6. Physical assault     _____
        7. Sexual assault     _____
        8. Other sexual misconduct     _____

          9. Vandalism               _____

         10. Other (specify: _____)     _____

   C.    Known history of involvement in criminal offenses.

          1. Drug possession         _____

          2. Drug dealing           _____

          3. Breaking and entering    _____

          4. Robbery (armed)        _____

          5. Robbery (unarmed)      _____

          6. Physical assault        _____

          7. Sexual assault         _____

          8. Other sexual misconduct   _____

          9. Vandalism            _____

         10. Other (specify: _____)     _____

   D.    Probation

          1. Is youth currently on probation?

          2. Has youth been on probation?

V.   Psychiatric Disturbance

   A.   Reason for concern

          1.  depression, withdrawal     _____

          2.  social isolation          _____

          3.  anxiety/general distress/nervousness/worrying _____

          4.  frequent conflict with peers   _____

          5.  odd, bizarre or disorganized behavior   _____

          6.  developmental disability/mental retardation   _____

          7.  mood lability           _____

          8.  victimization/exploitation by others   _____

          9.  other (specify: _____)     _____

VI.   Family problems

   A.   Reason for concern

          1.  neglect             _____

          2.  physical abuse          _____

          3.  sexual abuse           _____

          4.  emotional maltreatment     _____

          5.  parental substance abuse    _____

          6.  parental involvement in criminal activities   _____

          7.  custody/visitation conflict    _____

8. chronic domestic conflict                              _____
9. other (specify: _____)                            _____

## Case Disposition

Please describe your involvement in the above case beginning with the initial contact. Be certain to provide approximate number of sessions seen. An example is provided.

Example:
Initial contact was acute response, met with child and sibling.
Subsequently met with parent 3 times, and conducted 3 session follow-up assessment with child.
Referred child to CSC for long term follow-up.
She was assigned to Jane Smith.
Transfer was successful.

# CHILD DEVELOPMENT-COMMUNITY POLICING PROGRAM

## MONTHLY CASE SERVICE LOG

Clinician code: _____
Month/Year: _____

*Directions: Please record every CD/CP related activity using the available codes. Give this to the administrative assistant at the end of each month.*

| Case #* | Date | Description of Activity | Service Duration Hrs/Min | Travel Duration Hrs/Min | Activity Code | Service Code | Location Code | Clinicians Present | Officer Present |
|---------|------|------------------------|--------------------------|-------------------------|---------------|--------------|---------------|--------------------|-----------------|
| ___ | __/__ | _____ | _____ | _____ | F/T/C | _____ | _____ | _____ | Y/N |
| ___ | __/__ | _____ | _____ | _____ | F/T/C | _____ | _____ | _____ | Y/N |
| ___ | __/__ | _____ | _____ | _____ | F/T/C | _____ | _____ | _____ | Y/N |
| ___ | __/__ | _____ | _____ | _____ | F/T/C | _____ | _____ | _____ | Y/N |
| ___ | __/__ | _____ | _____ | _____ | F/T/C | _____ | _____ | _____ | Y/N |
| ___ | __/__ | _____ | _____ | _____ | F/T/C | _____ | _____ | _____ | Y/N |
| ___ | __/__ | _____ | _____ | _____ | F/T/C | _____ | _____ | _____ | Y/N |

**Case #:**
ID # of referral
If no ID #, put 999

**Activity Codes:**
F = face to face w/client
T = telephone contact
C = work without client

**Service Codes w/Patient:**
| | |
|---|---|
| Acute Response | 101 |
| Follow-up assessment | 102 |
| Individual therapy | 103 |
| Parent guidance | 104 |
| Parent/child therapy | 105 |
| Sibling/Peer therapy | 106 |
| Group therapy | 107 |
| Family therapy | 108 |

**Service Codes without Patient:**
| | |
|---|---|
| Contact with police | 201 |
| Contact with school | 202 |
| Contact with CSC clinician | 203 |
| Contact with YNHH staff | 204 |
| Contact with DCF | 205 |
| Contact with other agency | 206 |
| Paperwork | 301 |
| Supervision | 302 |

**Location Codes:**
| | |
|---|---|
| 1 = own home | |
| 2 = other home | |
| 3 = CSC | |
| 4 = school | |
| 5 = police headquarters | |
| 6 = police substation | |
| 7 = court | |
| 8 = hospital | |
| 9 = public place | |
| 10 = telephone | |
| 11 = other agency | |

**Clinician Codes:**
| | |
|---|---|
| 1 = Jean Adnopoz | |
| 2 = Miriam Berkman | |
| 3 = Steve Berkowitz | |
| 4 = Jim Canning | |
| 5 = Alice Colonna | |
| 6 = Steven Marans | |
| 7 = Mark Schaefer | |

*If multiple cases served during one activity, list additional case #'s and leave remainder blank

# References

American Psychiatric Association (1994). *Diagnostic and Statistical Manual of Mental Disorders*. 4th ed. Washington, D.C.: American Psychiatric Association.

Bowlby, J. (1988). *A Secure Base: Parent-Child Attachment and Healthy Human Development*. New York: Basic Books.

Brown, L. (1990). Inaugural Speech as Commissioner of Police of New York City (January 22).

Comer, J. P. (1980). *School Power: Implications of an Intervention Project*. Introduction by Albert J. Solnit and Samuel Nash. New York: Free Press; London: Collier Macmillan.

Comer, J. P., and Haynes, N. M. (1990). Helping Black Children Succeed: The Significance of Some Social Factors. In *Going to School:*

*The African American Experience*, K. Lomotey (ed.), pp. 103–112. New York: State University of New York Press.

Comer, J. P., Haynes, N. M., Anson, A. R., Cook, T. D., Habib, F., and Grady, M. K. (1991). The Comer School Development Program: A Theoretical Analysis. *Urban Education* 26 (1): 56–82.

Eck, J. E., and Spelman, W. (1987). *Problem-Solving: Problem-Oriented Policing in Newport News*. Washington, D.C.: Police Executive Research Forum.

Geller, W. (ed.) (1991). *Local Government Police Management*. Washington, D.C.: International City/County Management Association.

Goldstein, H. (1977). *Policing a Free Society*. Cambridge, Mass.: Ballinger.

———. (1990). *Problem-Oriented Policing*. Philadelphia: Temple University Press.

Goldstein, J., Freud, A., and Solnit, A. J. (1973). *Beyond the Best Interests of the Child*. New York: Free Press.

———. (1979). *Before the Best Interests of the Child*. New York: Free Press.

Goldstein, J., Freud, A., Solnit, A. J., and Goldstein, S. (1986). *In the Best Interests of the Child*. New York: Free Press.

Kelling, G. L. (1988a). The Quiet Revolution in American Policing. *Perspectives on Policing*, No. 1. Washington, D.C.: U.S. Department of Justice, Office of Justice Programs, National Institute of Justice.

———. (1988b). The Evolving Strategy of Policing. In *Perspectives on Policing Series*. U.S. Department of Justice and Program in Criminal Justice Policy and Management, Kennedy School of Government, Harvard University.

Knitzer, J., with the assistance of L. Olson. (1982). *Unclaimed Children: The Failure of Public Responsibility to Children and Adolescents in Need of Mental Health Services*. Washington, D.C.: Children's Defense Fund.

Marans, S. (1994). Community Violence and Children's Development: Collaborative Interventions. In *Children and Violence*, C. Chiland and G. Young (eds.), pp. 109–124. Northvale, N.J.: Jason Aronson.

Marans, S., Berkman, M., and Cohen, D. (In press). Communal Violence: Children's Development and Their Adaptations to Catastrophic Circumstances. In *Minefields in Their Hearts: The Mental*

*Health of Children in War and Communal Violence*, R. Apfel and B. Simon (eds.).

Marans, S., and Cohen, D. (1993). Children and Inner-City Violence: Strategies for Intervention. In *The Effects of War and Violence on Children*, L. Leavitt and N. Fox (eds.), pp. 218–301. Hillsdale, N.J.: Lawrence Erlbaum.

Martinez, P., and Richters, J. E. (1993). The NIMH Community Violence Project II: Children's Distress Symptoms Associated with Violence Exposure. *Psychiatry* 56: 22–35.

New Haven Public Schools. (1992). Report on the Social and Health Assessment. *Social Development Project Evaluation, 1991–92: Final Report.*

Pynoos, R. S., and Nader, K. (1988). Psychological First Aid and Treatment Approaches to Children Exposed to Community Violence: Research Implications. *Journal of Traumatic Stress* 1 (4): 445–473.

——. (1989). Children's Memory and Proximity to Violence. *Journal of the American Academy of Child and Adolescent Psychiatry* 28 (2): 236–241.

——. (1990). Children's Exposure to Violence and Traumatic Death. *Psychiatry Annals* 20 (6): 334–344.

Richters, J. E., and Martinez, P. (1993). The NIMH Community Violence Project I: Children as Victims of and Witnesses to Violence. *Psychiatry* 53: 7–21.

Robertson, J., and Robertson, J. (1969). *John, Seventeen Months, in Residential Nursery for Nine Days.* Distributed by New York University Film Library.

Singleton, J. (1991). *Boyz N the Hood.* Columbia Pictures.

Sparrow, M., Kennedy, D., and Moore, M. (1990). *Beyond 911: A New Era for Policing.*1 New York: Basic Books.

Surgeon General's Workshop on Violence and Public Health (1991). *Violence in America: A Public Health Approach*, M. Rosenberg and M. Fenley (eds.). Oxford: Oxford University Press.

Taylor, L., Zuckerman, B., Harik, V., and McAlister-Groves, B. (1994). Witnessing Violence by Young Children and Their Mothers. *Developmental and Behavioral Pediatrics Journal* 15 (2): 120–123.

Terr, L. C. (1989). Family Anxiety after Traumatic Events. *Journal of Clinical Psychiatry* 50 (11): 15–19.

———. (1991). Childhood Traumas: An Outline and Overview. *American Journal of Psychiatry* 148 (1): 10–20.

U.S. Department of Justice. (1993). Uniform Crime Reporting (UCR) — Crime in the United States. Washington, D.C.: Federal Bureau of Investigation.

# Index

Abuse: reporting, 47, 81, 83; versus neglect, 47

Adolescence, 42, 59–60; aggression in, 57, 59; early, 55–57; stress of, 56, 59

Aggression: in adolescents, 57, 59; as a response, 3

Anxiety, 5; developmental phase-specific, 112, 116, 119

Attachment difficulties, 49

Attention disorders, 3

Boston City Hospital: children and violence study, 4–5

Bowlby, John, 48

*Boyz N the Hood* (film), 60

Brown, Lee, 6

Budgetary considerations, 100–03

Case illustrations, 113–22

Case load (of clinicians), 79

Case review, 86–93

Case Service Log form, 138

CASSP (Child and Adolescent Services System Program), 9

CD-CP. *See* Child Development–Community Policing Program

Child and Adolescent Services System Program (CASSP), 9

Child development: police education in, 12, 13–14, 40, 42, 107. *See also* Child development phases

Child Development–Community Policing Program (CD-CP), 1–2; consultants from, 97, 98, 99; number of cases, 16; origin of, vii, 10, 104; purpose, 10–11, 105; results, 104–05, 108–09

Child development fellowships, 12, 19–24, 98; clinical rotations, 27–30; confidentiality during, 33–35; goals, 20; participants, 24; sample schedule, 28–29; training, 27–33

Child development phases: infancy, 45–48; 18 months to 3 years, 48–50; 4 to 6 years, 50–52; 7 to 11 years, 53–54; adolescence, 42, 55–57, 59–60

Children: high risk, 123; removal from home, 47

Child welfare authorities: criteria for reporting, 83; reports to, 47, 65, 67, 73, 83

Class issues, 58

Clinical interviews: confidentiality of, 80–82

Clinical practice: changes in, 109; house calls, 109

Clinical referrals, 65–66

Clinical rotations, 27–30

Clinical staff: criteria for, 26; on-call, 79

Clinician. *See* Mental health professional

Collaboration, ix, 1–2, 10, 16, 110; confidentiality and, 33–34, 80–82, 92; problem-solving, 94

Community: as focus, 10; police relationship with, 5–7, 11

Community-based policing, vii, 11; requirements for, 12, 107

Conferences, 15–16

Confidentiality, 33–35, 45, 80–82, 92; waiver form, 34, 35

Conflict of interest, 82; in criminal cases, 81

Consent: informed, 34

Consultation service, 14–15, 62; clinical referrals, 63, 65–66, 110; costs, 102–03; follow-up, 69, 103; interagency collaboration, 64, 67–69; officer support, 70; on-call resources, 63; operating procedures, 71; referrals to, 71–72, 74; staffing, 24

Coordination: program, 64, 84, 100

Coping skills (of children), 51,
    53–54
Costs (program), 100–03
Criminal cases: confidentiality, 81
Crying, excessive: as symptom, 49

Data: information to record, 99–
    100
Delinquent behavior: adolescent,
    57; as reaction to violence,
    3–4
Depression: in children, 5, 49, 50;
Deterrence: emphasis on, 7
Developmental phase-specific anx-
    ieties, 112, 116, 119
*DSM-IV*, 3

Eating disturbances, 3, 46, 49, 54

Family development, 41
Fantasies (of children), 52, 54,
    56; intervention, 112, 122
Fearfulness: as symptom, 3, 5
Fellows (in CD-CP), 12, 20, 98,
    101, 102; criteria for, 25.
    *See also* Child development
    fellowships
Flashbacks: as symptom, 3
Follow-up (by clinicians with po-
    lice), 78
Follow-up home visits, 69, 103,
    109: recovery and, 110
Framingham (Mass.): CD-CP
    evaluation study, 100

Gang issues, 72
Guns: as intimidating, 28

Hospitals: police exposure to, 30
House calls (by clinicians), 15,
    109
Human behavior: police training
    in, 13, 40, 107

Infancy: key concepts, 45–46
Interagency collaboration, ix, 67,
    107–08; confidentiality
    and, 92
Intervention, 10, 14, 52, 123;
    early, viii, 7, 11, 12, 52;
    short-term, 79
Interviews: sample forms, 125–29

*John* (film), 50
Joint Commission on Mental
    Health of Children: 1970
    report of, 9
Juvenile detention facility: visits
    to, 21–22, 30

Kelling, George L., 5
Knitzer, J., 9

Leadership, 100. *See also* Staff

Mental health professionals: case
    load, 79; changes for, 8–9,
    11, 109–10; as consultants,
    10, 15, 38, 82; consulta-
    tion/supervision, 79–80;
    house calls, 15, 109; issues,
    36; learn about police, viii,
    ix, 12–13, 23–24, 30–33,
    36; on-call, 15, 63–64; pro-
    gram participants, 26; refer-

Mental health professionals (*cont.*)
rals to, 65–66, 71, 75–76;
roles, 8, 10, 11; therapeutic
neutrality, 35. *See also* Staff,
clinical
Mental health resources, 60–61
Mother-child relationship, 46
Mothers: hostile/defensive, 47

National Institute of Mental
Health, 9
Neglect: versus abuse, 47
New Haven CD-CP Program:
origin of, vii, 10, 104; results, 104–05, 108–09
New Haven Department of Police
Service, 10, 100: CD-CP
program in, 104–05;
community-based approach,
vii

Officer support, 70
Outpatient clinic: training in, 29

Parenting: child's needs and, 46
Patients: informed consent of, 34
Peer pressure: for adolescents, 56;
for children, 53
Play: as expressive, 50
Police: attitudes of, 42, 100, 106–
08; attitudes toward, 8, 53;
changes in, 17; changing
backgrounds of, 13; 105–
08; education of, ix, 2, 11,
12, 13–14, 19–22, 40–41,
101, 107; follow-up by, 69,
103, 110; follow-up with,
78; life experiences of, 22,
57; as role models, 14;
roles, viii–ix, 2, 7, 11, 117;
support for, 70–71; uni-
forms as intimidating, 38
Police Fellowship for Clinical Faculty, 12–13, 101
Policing: changing patterns of, 5–
7; community-based, vii, ix,
6–7, 11
Policy recommendations: by program conference, 95
Post-traumatic stress disorder, 3;
questionnaire, 125–29
Problem-solving: conferences, 15–
16; consultations, 14
Professional boundaries, 80
Program conference, 15–16, 84–
86, 99; administration, 95;
case review, 86–93; costs,
102; policy recommenda-
tions by, 95; problem solving, 94; program
integration, 93–94
Program development, 96; implementation, 99; initial, 97–
98; institutional investment,
97
Protocol, 99, 107
Psychiatric inpatient service: police
exposure to, 30
Puberty: as development stage, 55
Public schools: police exposure to,
30
Pynoos, R.S., 112

Questionnaires: for family, 125–29

Race issues, 58

Racial composition (of children), viii

Records: data to record, 99–100

Recovery: follow-up visits and, 110

Referrals, 15, 110; clinical, 65–66; criteria, 71–72; emergency, 65, 73; form for, 76–77; nonemergency, 74; process of, 73

Report form (CD-CP), 130–37

Research opportunities, 100

Ride-alongs (with police), 12, 23–24, 31–32, 36; waiver of liability, 36–37

Risk: children at, 123; physical and emotional, 50

Robertson, James and Joyce, 50

Roles, definition of (in program), 82

Security: child's need for, 48

Self: adolescent reorganization of, 56

Separation and trauma, 48–50

Sexual development, 55–56, 59

Singleton, John, 60

Sleeping disturbances, 3, 46, 49, 54

Socioeconomic status, 58

Staff (CD-CP), 100, 101

Staff (clinical): criteria, 26; on-call, 79; short-term intervention, 79

Stress, 3, 51, 53–54. *See also* Trauma

Training seminars, 40; atmosphere, 44–45, 47; costs, 101; goals, 41–42; leaders, 41; outline, 42–43; size, 41, 101

Trauma: children's coping skills, 51, 53–54; effect on children, 49, 51, 111, 112–13; police awareness of, 106; symptoms, 3, 54, 112

Uniforms (police): as intimidating, 38

Violence, 1, 2–3; awareness of effects, 75; children's reactions to, 3–4, 77, 111–12; statistics on, 4–5

Waivers: on confidentiality, 34–35; for ride-alongs, 36–37

Witnesses, children as, 54

Yale Child Study Center, vii, 10, 100